They Were Eyewitnesses

They Were Eyewitnesses

Defending the Faith Like the Ancient Church

Nancy A. Almodovar

RESOURCE *Publications* • Eugene, Oregon

THEY WERE EYEWITNESSES
Defending the Faith Like the Ancient Church

Copyright © 2021 Nancy A. Almodovar. All rights reserved. Except for brief quotations in critical publications or reviews, no part of this book may be reproduced in any manner without prior written permission from the publisher. Write: Permissions, Wipf and Stock Publishers, 199 W. 8th Ave., Suite 3, Eugene, OR 97401.

Resource Publications
An Imprint of Wipf and Stock Publishers
199 W. 8th Ave., Suite 3
Eugene, OR 97401

www.wipfandstock.com

PAPERBACK ISBN: 978-1-7252-9879-8
HARDCOVER ISBN: 978-1-7252-9880-4
EBOOK ISBN: 978-1-7252-9881-1

07/14/21

Scripture quotations are taken from The ESV® Bible (The Holy Bible, English Standard Version®), copyright © 2001 by Crossway, a publishing ministry of Good News Publishers. Used by permission. All rights reserved.

I did nothing.
The Word of God did everything.

—MARTIN LUTHER

Contents

Preface | ix
Acknowledgments | xi
Introduction | xiii

1. Just the Facts, Please! | 1
2. Crooked Foundations | 6
3. Objective Evidence | 14
4. A Pattern Recovered | 18
5. Peter Sets the Pattern | 29
6. Following the Apostles | 34
7. Proclaiming the Name of Jesus | 40
8. Deathbed Testimony | 43
9. The One Who Died and Now Lives Gives Life | 47
10. Not Done in a Corner | 52
11. To the World | 57
12. Recovering the Apostles' Apologetic | 63

Epilogue | 69
Resources | 71

Preface

"Do you have any eyewitnesses?" That is the question the courts go to when reviewing a case. Many times, eyewitness accounts are taken down by the first officers on the scene, and those statements are as good as if the person comes to court and testifies. Written statements or affidavits are equally as valid as the people telling the account themselves. Deathbed accounts tend to have even more weight placed on them for their truthfulness, because it is assumed that the person doesn't want to enter the afterlife as a liar. So the questions are as follows: "Does the New Testament have any eyewitnesses?" "Are they reliable?" "Are they verifiable?" "Were they written down?" "How specific are they? Are places, times, events, and people spoken of in their statements who would have been able to validate their message?" Absolutely! It is these eyewitnesses that will be looked into in this apologetic book along with the pattern they set for both proclaiming and defending the Christian faith.

The title of this book emphasizes that they (the apostles and evangelists) were the eyewitnesses, just as Peter states in his sermon to Cornelius and his household:

> And we are witnesses of all that he did both in the country of the Jews and in Jerusalem. They put him to death by hanging him on a tree, but God raised him on the third day. (Acts 10:39–40)

Since it was the evangelists and apostles who were the eyewitnesses and not us, we contemporary believers are to bring *their*

Preface

testimony to the conversation. We are not to be going around telling about our inner experiences, but rather the public testimony and record of the apostles and evangelists. This book will show you how they proclaimed and defended the gospel, and it is my prayer that it will become your pattern as you tell others the good news that Jesus died, was buried, and rose again, according to the Scriptures.

Acknowledgments
In Gratitude

WHEN I BEGAN MY studies at Trinity Theological Bible College in Newburgh, Indiana, I had no idea how God would providentially lead me out of the study of biblical counseling into the fields of apologetics and theology. There, via the online courses, I first met Dr. John Warwick Montgomery. It was in that first class that I finally understood why, when any sermon was preached, my instinct was to ask, "Where is that in the Bible?" Through his apologetics courses over the next eight years (bachelor of arts to master of arts in apologetics), I learned that we have a faith which is defensible, has verifiable facts, and is the only objective truth in this world.

To the ladies at Faith Lutheran Church in Mountain Home, Idaho, for your seeing in me something that needed to be further trained so that others can know the assurance and comfort of the objective and only truth of the Christian faith, thank you for supporting me, sending me to the International Academy, helping defray the costs of the many books and research papers I would need, and mostly for giving your love, friendship, and encouragement. You first noticed that the spark to tell others of the love of God in Christ had waned under the austerity of Calvinism's teaching of election and reprobation, and it was you who took up the gauntlet to fan the flame which remained. Ignited once again with a desire

Acknowledgments

to proclaim him who was alive, crucified, died, and is alive again forevermore, I am truly indebted to you for all you have done.

To my brother-in-law, Kenneth Adams, who gifted me with the *Ancient Church Commentary,* which allowed me to see how these sermons in Acts were used to both proclaim and defend the faith. A timely gift which clearly showed prescience on Ken's part.

To the men and women who attend my weekly Zoom apologetics course, thank you for your support and encouragement. Certain events may have initially separated us, but in God's providence, we were given an opportunity to learn from his Word how we should both proclaim and defend the faith. (To attend my *free* apologetics courses, fill out the contact form at www.lutherangirl.org or email me at drnancyalmodovar@gmail.com.)

Finally to my husband, Roberto, affectionately called Bobby, this book is dedicated to you. Your response to my questions has always been: "What do the Scriptures say?" Thank you for your wisdom and love. I know you spent much time praying for me that God would give me wisdom to handle this topic, being faithful to God's Word, and I love you for that. Your love for me, your desire to see me succeed in whatever endeavor I took on, means so much to me and is a driving force within me. Thank you. I love you.

Introduction

Imagine if you will the following scenario:

Your doorbell rings, and as you open the door you find two very nice young adults standing there offering you material to read. You take it graciously and begin to scan and see that they are here at your home to introduce you to their religion. You read the material and begin to ask them this very important question, "How do you know your religion is the true one?"

Their typical response is this, "We know it's true because we can feel it in our heart."

You respond, "That's fascinating because I too believe that my religion is true because I can feel it in my heart."

You are now at a standoff. Which subjective testimony is true? Which one is the truth?

IF THIS SCENARIO SOUNDS familiar, it probably is, because you were taught that knowing whether something is true is based on subjective feelings or experiences or both. Yet how do you, as a Christian, counter the subjective truth of another religion if all you know is the subjective truth of your own religion?

You see, Christianity is not about your feelings or experiences but about the historical events that happened in the lifetimes of the apostles and evangelists fulfilling what the prophets spoke of in the Scripture. Christianity is the only objective religion. Christianity is the only religion that looks to evidence and eyewitness testimony within a specific historic place and time. Though many, especially since the 1800s, have looked inwardly for proof of God,

Introduction

it is objective truth that Christianity stands upon for validation. Feelings come and go, but actual historic events and people do not. Christianity alone brings objective truth to a world stuck on personal testimony and experience. Christianity is the only religion which can be validated, not on the basis of the subjective but on the objective. As Simon Greenleaf writes,

> The foundation of our religion is a basis of fact—the fact of the birth, ministry, miracles, death, resurrection by the Evangelists as having actually occurred, within their own personal knowledge.[1]

If those of another religion are basing the validity and veracity of their beliefs on how it makes them feel, and you respond in kind, then you have given up the true arguments and defenses for the Christian faith. You have made Christianity to trip and fall on the exact same faulty foundation as every other religion. Christianity then becomes no different from any other religion. In reality, you have failed to present the Christian faith in the biblical and apostolic manner. Christianity is based upon eyewitness testimony of specific people, in specific places, recounting specific public events, which did not happen in a dream nor, as St. Paul says, "in a corner" (Acts 26:26) or in secret. Rather, Christianity is the only religion which has historical and eyewitness facts on its side.

Certainly, when the unbelieving, spiritual, or religious person comes to your door or engages you in conversation in the marketplace, you cannot simply say, "Well, I believe what my church teaches..." You must have an answer for him or her, since that is what Scripture requires, "always being prepared to make a defense to anyone who asks you for a reason for the hope that is in you " (1 Pet 3:15). We are to be equipped to answer and ready to respond with the gospel of Jesus Christ the way the apostles and evangelists were.

What do you say? How do you respond? If your own personal experience does not prove the religion objectively true, where do you go? What is your answer to their questions? To whom or what

---

1. Greenleaf, "Testimony of the Evangelists."

Introduction

do you appeal? These are the questions that remain when we find that subjective, personal experiences do not prove Christianity true. Where do we go? We go to the eyewitnesses and the documentary evidence in the Word of God. This is where you find the objective truth as you sit on the stand in the court of popular opinion and deliver the testimony of the evangelists, not your personal one.

The apostles never presented their experiences or feelings as proof except that to which they were eyewitnesses. This book walks through the many sermons of the evangelists and Paul in the book of Acts to show the reader that the best apologetic for the Christian faith is found in the objective evidence for it. While even the apostles may begin their proclamation and defense of the Christian faith with what they personally saw, they quickly move on to the historic events and eyewitness testimony. The apostles and evangelists may share their personal experiences, but that is because the events happened in the context of their own lives and they were there, at those events, listening to Jesus teach, seeing the miracles and the crucifixion, death, and resurrection of Jesus himself. You and I were not. Therefore, we are not eyewitnesses to these things as they were eyewitnesses.

Sit at the feet of the apostles reading their sermons as recorded in the book of Acts, and you find that they appeal to historic events to which they were the eyewitnesses. These men do not even appeal to their own feelings or experiences but rather to the facts that these things—the death, burial, and resurrection of Jesus—actually occurred "within their own personal knowledge"[2] and many times even within the knowledge and experiences of their accusers. They do not rely upon their own experiences/testimony, however grand they may have been (think of the transfiguration of Jesus in front of Peter, James, and John), but upon the Scriptures, the prophecies and fulfillment of them all in Jesus Christ, Son of God and Son of Man. This is where Christians must go if we are to make a proper defense of the gospel, because God promised his Word does not return void (Isa 55:11).

---

2. Greenleaf, "Testimony of the Evangelists."

Introduction

The good news about this type of defense for the faith is that Christians have objective truth. Christians have historical facts, documentary evidence, eyewitness testimony, and so much more to prove that the Christian faith is the only true religion. Are you complaining about using objective proofs? Are you saying, "But the apostles used experience and so should we"? What if I told you that even the apostle Peter said we have a more faithful record in what is written by the prophets and apostles than even that which he experienced?

> But we were eyewitnesses of his majesty.... We ourselves heard this very voice borne from heaven, for we were with him on the holy mountain. And we have something more sure, the prophetic word, to which you will do well to pay attention as to a lamp shining in a dark place. (2 Pet 1:16b–19)

Christians today do not hear the voice of God the Father speak directly from the "Majestic Glory," for in these days God speaks to us through his Son (Heb 11:2). No one alive today, or since the days of the apostles and first-century Christians, has seen the risen Christ. None of us were eyewitnesses to his life, death, burial and physical resurrection from the dead. Therefore, if we are defending the gospel, we must appeal to the eyewitnesses. This is the more sure prophetic word and is, in fact, the gospel that is the power of God for salvation (Rom 1:16).

You will learn in this book the simple pattern that the apostles set forth when they were questioned about their Christian faith. In each sermon outlined here you will find that Peter, John, Stephen, and Paul all use a similar pattern to both proclaim and defend the Christian faith.

It is my hope then that the reader will come to learn and appreciate the way the apostles did apologetics and gospel proclamation and utilize it within his or her own discussions and conversations with unbelievers and skeptics alike. Utilizing our testimonies should be only a starting point and we, like the apostles, should move off of them as quickly as possible. No testimony ever saved anybody. The object, Jesus Christ, is the one who redeems us.

Introduction

So please join me as we explore sermons found in the book of Acts given both in defense and proclamation of the good news that Jesus Christ died for the sins of the world, so that those who believe may have everlasting life. Amen.

Therefore, we go to the apostles, because *they were eyewitnesses*!

1

Just the Facts, Please!

"Nancy, why are you a Christian? Why do you go to church on Sundays and even during the week?" This is where the conversation begins. These are, in fact, the very questions I have been asked in the past by neighbors, friends, and family. How do you respond to family, neighbors, or co-workers when they ask about your faith? Do you know how to respond? Do you, as Peter tells us, have an answer (*apologia*) "for the hope that is in you" (1 Pet 3:15)?

If you are like most evangelical Christians, you end up giving them your personal testimony. You share how you came to believe in Jesus, made a decision for him, gave your heart to Jesus, or one of the other many various ways modern Christianity describes conversion. Is this, though, the way the evangelists and apostles spoke about their belief in Jesus Christ? No! They stuck with the facts—just the facts. This is where our journey begins in learning to defend the faith using eyewitness accounts and documentary evidences.

When talking with others about the Christian faith, rather than looking at our own subjective experiences, we should and must go to the eyewitnesses. As Simon Greenleaf says,

> The foundation of our religion is a basis of facts—the fact of the birth, ministry, miracles, death, resurrection by

the Evangelists as having actually occurred, within their own personal knowledge.[1]

The life, death, and resurrection of Jesus Christ did not occur during your lifetime, and you are not an eyewitness. However, when speaking with unbelievers and skeptics, keeping our conversation based upon the eyewitnesses' testimony, found in the New Testament, will result in objective truth offered rather than your own subjective feelings, opinions, and experiences. This keeps the conversation on the facts and the message given to us in the Scripture, and that is where the power of the gospel lies. Offering opinion will collide with the opinions of others. However, offering just the facts will cause people to face them and either walk away in their own stubborn unbelief or respond in true faith, through the power of the Holy Spirit working through his Word. As Christians defending the faith, it is the eyewitness testimony to which we must appeal.

When one bases truth on personal experiences, rather than upon the objective truth of the Word of God, the presentation becomes egocentric instead of Christocentric. This type of proclamation takes away the glory, authority, and veracity from God and leans too much on human experiences as a way to prove it. As Dr. Montgomery says in his lecture "Christianity in a Corner":

> The preaching of Scripture needs to focus on the heart of the Scriptures.[2]

Yes, God has saved you from great peril and sin, but that is not to be the focal point of the proclamation. Rather, the point of a gospel presentation is, well, the gospel, for it "is the power of God unto salvation" (Rom 1:16). Forgiveness of sins and freedom from sin, death, and the devil are found in the gospel first. While God makes use of the foolishness of preaching to bring about saving faith, new birth, and eternal life, what we proclaim should not be about ourselves. In a recent conversation with my own sister, we discussed how varied conversion stories are. Her own is one that is

1. Greenleaf, "Testimony of the Evangelists."
2. Montgomery, "Christianity in a Corner," 34:50.

Just the Facts, Please!

quiet, as God was working in a subtle way with her. However my own story is one of drastic, cataclysmic change. My family, friends, and co-workers were shocked to find me reading the Bible; my own boss at that time thought I had had a mental breakdown and offered to send me to his psychiatrist. I tried to explain to him that the complete 180° turn in my life was because Jesus had saved me. Later on I would find out that salvation had happened on the cross, but even when I had incorrect theology, I understood Jesus had given me a new heart, one where I wanted to love and serve him. What I had experienced was the forgiveness of sins, and I longed to tell everyone about this.

The problem I had was that I would share what had happened to me on that Tuesday night in September 1986 instead of the objective facts found in the New Testament. It had been such a drastic conversion that I just wanted to tell everyone about my experience. Back to the conversation with my sister: we talked about how by sharing our conversion story as adults, it could make the hearer long for a radical conversion experience. The result is the focus is on my personal testimony instead of on the eyewitness accounts given to us in the New Testament. If I put too much weight on what I subjectively experience, the result is that my testimony overtakes the objective truths found in the Word of God.

Understanding that the Christian church has been gifted with an objective gospel, one not based on feelings or emotions as evidence of the truth of the life, death, and resurrection of Jesus Christ, I want to challenge my evangelical friends to proclaim the objective truth of God to others, whether or not they feel it that day. No longer should we be testifying "I know he lives, because he lives within my heart,"[3] but rather, "I know he lives, because Christ died for our sins in accordance with the Scriptures, 'that he was buried, that he was raised on the third day in accordance with the Scriptures'" (1 Cor 15: 3b–4).

This is where the power of God lies: through the weakness and "foolishness of preaching" (1 Cor 1:21), not in the flamboyance of your testimony. The authority of the message of Christianity does

---

3. See, for example, Ackley, "I Serve a Risen Savior."

not lie in experiences or feelings, the "hope-so's" or "think-so's" but rather in the facts, the objective truths, which are: Jesus lived, died, and rose again to bring life to all who would believe.

Only with a recovery of this truth, the objective message borne through the testimony of the eyewitnesses, can we hope to bring to the lost a proper gospel proclamation. Christians should be helped to realize that while personal testimony has its place, that place is not the pinnacle or focal point of the message. Christians must ever keep in the forefront of their thoughts, while proclaiming or defending the faith, that their personal testimony does not save anyone. God says in his Word that the gospel "is the power . . . unto salvation" (Rom 1:16–17). Using the same pattern found in the book of Acts, in the sermons of the apostles and a deacon (Stephen), will bring true power back to evangelism. Enabling people to see the weaknesses of a subjective faith will be the only way to move them away from a debilitated gospel to God's strong Word.

A subjective gospel will continue to devastate the growth and health of the church and wreck the witness we have to Christ. A subjective gospel will limit the effect of the message and is limited to one's own experience. Instead, the objective gospel presentation is not focused on religious enthusiasm, but presents truths which challenge the unbeliever and skeptic to face the verifiable truths of the life, death, and resurrection of Christ. Brings the unbeliever straight to that door of salvation on which hangs "Whosoever will may enter." It removes unbelievers' objections to the demonstrable proofs of the physical resurrection of Jesus and forces them to humble themselves and believe whether or not Jesus is who he said or if they would prefer to remain in their sins.

This is not a trifling matter. Getting the gospel right is paramount to the church doing the task Jesus gave us: to proclaim him to all, baptizing and making disciples. This book is not saying to get all your theology systematized and in a neat box; rather, it is about the gospel and proclaiming that message. Friedrich Schiller, in his *Philosophical Letters*, writes, "Rarely do we arrive at the summit of truth without running into extremes; we have frequently to exhaust the part of error, and even of folly, before we work our way up to the noble goal of tranquil wisdom."[4] It behooves the believer to run from past error, give up extremes and subjectivism which turn the gospel into a message of our own making, and return to the gospel, being about the life, death, and resurrection of Jesus Christ.

The church has battled subjectivism for two millennia Martin Luther also had to face the little corruptions that seep into the church, as when he penned this hymn:

> Lord, keep us steadfast in Your Word;
> Curb those who by deceit or sword
> Would wrest the kingdom from Your Son
> And bring to naught all He has done.[5]

A gospel proclamation based upon what one feels or thinks will never save. Instead, God has promised us in his Word that the gospel, the objective truth of the life, death, and resurrection of God's own Son Jesus Christ, is the "power of God unto salvation." May God grant his church the clarity to stop proclaiming the minute doctrinal peculiarities of our denominations and preach the pure Word of God, the gospel of the kingdom of his own dear Son, our risen Savior, Jesus Christ.

In the book *Praying Luther's Small Catechism*, Werner Klein writes in the foreword,

> that the Church must never be found wanting in proclaiming the declaration of forgiveness and salvation in Christ.[6]

This, my brothers and sisters in Christ, is what we are to proclaim: Christ died for your sins. We do this by proclaiming what the apostles and evangelists wrote down in Scripture, since *they were eyewitnesses.*

---

4. Schiller, *Schiller's Philosophical Letters*, 21.
5. Luther, "Lord, Keep Us Steadfast."
6. Werner Klein in Pless, *Praying Luther's Small Catechism*, vii.

2

Crooked Foundations

Killing the Bible

Dr. Montgomery taught in his lectures in Strasbourg, France, that in the eighteenth century, "the Bible was killed." The objective truths of the holy Scriptures were questioned, and subjective opinion was elevated. The question which should be asked is whether the liberal move to "kill the Bible" created the vacuum in churches to hear God's voice outside of the Bible. Did the liberal move to kill the Bible leave a vacuum into which personal testimony replaced the eyewitness testimony of the evangelists? Did the diminishing of the need for the written word of God create an overemphasis on the eyewitnesses?

Christians need the written word of God, because that is where the eyewitnesses accounts are given. Any presentation of Jesus based upon one's own feelings and subjective experiences instead of upon the testimony of the prophets and apostles elevates the individual above God's word. Does using your personal testimony to such a degree that you almost forget to bring in the Word of God result in believers themselves killing the necessity of the Bible? Sometimes, yes. Christians need to utilize the written word of God in their apologetic endeavors, because that is where the true and powerful objective gospel is proclaimed best. Since we contemporary believers were not eyewitnesses to the events of the New Testament, we must rely upon the testimony of the evangelists who are the eyewitnesses.

Religious experience becomes the test of truth. Wesley's focus upon experience instead of the objective promises of God becomes the basis for his assurance of salvation. However, if one bases truth upon subjective experience, how does one rightfully challenge the experiences of a Muslim or Mormon, a Hindu or Sikh? If a person's subjective experience, the viability of which cannot be objectively verified, is the basis of truth, then we relinquish the right to say Christianity is true and all other religions false. Craig Parton writes, "Religious experience does not determine truth."[1] Just because you had an experience does not make your religion true. There must be valid objective evidence to the truth of a religion, or it becomes what every other religion and cult are: subjective belief systems and worldviews. A personal testimony is just that—personal. While it may be a starting point for presenting the gospel, it is not made to be how you defend the faith.

Unless there is an objective truth test, one cannot rightly state that his or her truth is true without objective evidence. If then your own experience becomes the foundation of your faith, when you no longer have those experiences, what happens with your faith? What then happens to those whom you proclaimed Christ to vis-à-vis experiences and personal testimony? When attacks against those subjective experiences are fostered, how does one battle for objective truth when one's own faith was never based upon facts and the testimony of eyewitnesses?

The modern evangelical reliance upon emotional interpretation, experiential learning, and basing truths on a gut instinct is all subjective. Truth, however, is not subjective but objective. The Word of God does not need your personal experience to validate it. In fact, the gospel has validated itself by its own internal truth tests, testimonies of eyewitness accounts, and fulfilled prophecies. Emotions which ebb and flow do not serve well as a foundation upon which Christianity stands or falls. Rather, the Scriptures

---

1. Parton, *Religion on Trial*, 29.

themselves give us the foundation and pillars of the church when they remind us that the "household of God is built on the foundation of the apostles and prophets" (Eph 2:20).

The result of having based gospel truth upon personal experiences and feelings was inevitable: a void of authority for the believer. Believers may have tried to test their experiences against Scripture, but it was a test from their own bad theology. That resulted in this void of authority, and in walked a restored apostolic and prophetic office.

It may sound very basic, but sometimes the simplest question is what gets people thinking critically about what they have been taught and they themselves have believed. As the wife of a master cabinet maker, I was taught by my husband that if the foundation is off by even a quarter of an inch, the wall will eventually fall and take down the building, resulting in injury and even death. Applying this concept of a strong and correct foundation is important to Scripture and the gospel proclamation.

Personal Experience as Proof

Many Christians use the phrase "God told me" to explain their plans in their day-to-day life. Many Evangelicals and even those who would not label themselves that way speak of God telling them directly what job to take, whom to marry, where to travel, etc. This subjective voice of God many times results in backtracking by believers when things do not pan out as they said God had told them it would.

Many believe a preacher or teacher because they "feel good," regardless of whether or not what the preacher or teacher says is found in the Bible. They view believing in Jesus as a "leap of faith." In my own experience, I know a preacher from the Wilson Avenue Mission in Brooklyn who says that he was "trying Jesus to see whether or not He was real." Others have said they would take their own feelings of peace and love over a stack of Bibles and doctrine. Many are moved by the music and excitement, claiming to "feel the Spirit moving." Preferring "mountain top experiences" rather than the simplicity of the Word and Sacraments. Perhaps they prayed for healing or some other need, and it was answered, so that they then believe. They may even have had a deep emotional experience and believed they were "led" to a certain place at a certain time and therefore, they became a Christian. Still other preachers tell the audience to pray until they can feel Christ in them and experience peace which "flows like a river." The end result for many is that their belief system is based upon their own feelings and experiences rather than on the objective truth of Jesus Christ.

Negative Effects

The effect on gospel proclamation is to lay Christianity side by side with every other religion. All world religions and their cults are based upon a personal experience or worldview, and none others have historical authentication that their beliefs are true. None have fulfilled prophecies or eyewitness testimony which has been recorded. Many do not even have archeological proofs which back the historical accounts as Christianity does. What other religions have are experiences that cannot be verified. Many of the ancient religions, such as Hinduism and Buddhism, have uncorroborated accounts, or their writings were more than two generations away from the events they claim to have occurred. Christianity stands above all of these world religions, but you need to move as quickly as possible away from a personal testimony or experience you had. Christianity is above all these religions, because it is historical and based upon objective events written by the eyewitnesses or those who worked side by side with them, such as in Luke and Mark's case. Relinquish this position for a subjective presentation, and you lay Christianity side by side, equal to, other religions. Bring in your subjective experiences, and Christianity is no truer than any other religion.

Attempts to defend Christianity based upon your subjective experience(s) results in the inability to say Christianity stands distinctly separate. Those Mormon missionaries at your door have an experience too: burning of the bosom. This informs them that their religion is true, and that's why they are there to share it with you. That experience is what directs them, and unless you present Christianity based upon objective truths, they will leave thinking you have your experience and they have theirs. Defending the faith requires that we realize our experiences do not mean much in light of the historic and documented proofs God has given to us. Your experiences are like straw in comparison to the gold, silver, and precious stones with which God gifted his church to proclaim him crucified and risen again, just as the Scriptures foretold.

Experience Is My/Our Creed

Rather than looking at what the Scriptures say, many Evangelicals will go by their gut, their intuition, and state that this is God telling them what to do or say. Many in the earliest years of the Pentecostal movement made this subjective word their guiding light. Early Evangelicals defined their movement as rethinking the Christian faith in light of their new experience of God rather than on the objective written Word. Instead of the Christian faith being founded upon objective truth and eyewitness testimony, it is based upon the experiences of the individual.

A false modern apostle reminds us:

> Testimonies are great but you need to invite them to "come and see" for themselves. They need to experience Jesus through visions, dreams and the anointing they receive. To prove to them Jesus is the Way they must experience Him in their personal lives through the anointing (modern day prophets, seers and visions).[2]

He continues to teach, "They will not remain Christians for long if God does not excite them to follow him through these various anointings."[3] Without experiences, the modern Pentecostals hold that the proclamation of the gospel is hindered. They also believe that without miracles and charismatic experiences, the

2. Lehman, "Come Unto Jesus."
3. Lehman, "Come Unto Jesus."

effect of that proclamation will eventually fade away. Without excitement and personal experiences, those who once believed will fall away.

This idea that truth is established through personal experiences and feelings must be challenged. If the gospel is about how you feel one day, but the next you don't feel or experience it, then the gospel is nothing more than fairy tales. This emphasis on experience, in a gospel presentation, results in the gospel's effectiveness being based upon the individual rather than, as God says, upon "the gospel [as] the power of God unto salvation." It is not based upon experience, though certainly we all do personally experience forgiveness and grace; but it is based upon objective truth, which results in sinners being declared justified. It is the notion which both Martin Luther and later C. F. W. Walter expressed as an *intra nos* focus versus *extra nos*.

The *intra nos* focus brings with it great defects to the presentation of the gospel testimony. If the believer is to proclaim some experience within (*intra nos*) over and against the testimony of Scripture (*extra nos*), the results are debilitating. For the believer, those feelings change all the time. No one, if they are honest, feels "saved" all the time. The struggle with sin alone from within and without brings damning charges. Even St. Paul writes about them when he cries out, "Who will deliver me" (Rom 7:24). The world, the devil, and our sinful self constantly contradict us when we rely upon experiences as the foundation on which we stand for assurance. If then believers who rely upon subjective experiences cannot be sure of their salvation, how will any to whom we proclaim this subjective religion ever be assured that their sins are forgiven and they too will live eternally? They cannot.

A religion based upon experience and personal testimony "over dogma and doctrine"[4] will result in either pride or depression. If based on and kept by pride, pride in one's testimony and experiences, it will fall. However, most believers who base their assurance on their experience will, in fact, at some point begin to question their salvation and struggle with spiritual depression. All religions

4. Jacobsen, *Thinking in the Spirit*, 6.

based upon an experiential model result in requiring things to obey and law to keep up with the next anointing and experience. This destroys assurance of faith and calls into question the reality of justification by faith alone based upon the resurrection of Jesus. It stands on a faulty foundation laid on emotions, which can be manipulated; whereas the truth of the gospel, in its properly proclaimed form, is based upon eyewitness testimony, validated by fulfilled prophecies of the Old Testament saints, according to the Scriptures.

This idea that experience permeates a gospel presentation is not left to the early Evangelicals or the latter charismatics and Third Wave movement but continues today. In a series titled "Come Unto Jesus," Pastor Roger Lehman teaches that "the church has focused too much on Christ as priest and the topics of forgiveness of sin, salvation, grace, etc."[5] Furthermore, he infers that when Jesus preached the gospel of the kingdom, there were miracles, deliverances, and healings, and so must we have today.

J. P. Moreland agrees with early Evangelicals that in order for the proclamation of the gospel to be successful, one of the three things needed is a "restoration of miraculous power."[6] A "power Gospel"[7] is what is promoted over and above the written testimony of prophets and apostles, and if those miraculous gifts are missing, the mission will fail. It is the idea that miracles, which were used by God to authenticate the mission, ministry, and message of the resurrection of Jesus for salvation, are to be utilized today, in order for people to believe the message. It places the experiences of current believers to a level of proof that should be held only by the Scriptures.

Moreland echoes the reasoning behind this supernatural necessity in gospel proclamation not on the Word of God but on his experience. He writes, "I have changed dramatically in recent years regarding what I have seen, heard, and done.... This period of growth has been the most moving, wonderful, impact-full [*sic*]

---

5. Lehman, "Come Unto Jesus."
6. Moreland, *Kingdom Triangle*, 181.
7. Lehman, "Come Unto Jesus."

time in my thirty-seven years of being a Christian.⁸" For Moreland and other modern Evangelicals, the effectiveness of gospel proclamation is about "becoming more effective colaborers with God in the Great Commission enterprise."⁹ His conclusion is that in order for the gospel to be effective, one must work in the supernatural and proclaim those supernatural experiences. It is in those experiences that belief is fostered and the church grows, according to modern Evangelicals.

There are several questions which should be asked, revolving around the 1800-plus years of the church when there was not an eschatological view that a restoration of the offices of prophets and apostles was needed to usher in the second coming of our Lord. What was the message proclaimed? How did the church grow from the one hundred twenty in the upper room to permeate the Roman Empire after their deaths? What caused the church to grow to the point we are at, where nearly in every nation there are believers? How did the church ever grow without the miraculous signs and experiences? How did the church ever get along with only the written Word?

For Moreland and those in his theological wheelhouse, he teaches that "merely exhorting people to believe things is ineffective."[10] For him, unless you have the miraculous happening, no one will believe. Is this what history bears out and witnesses to? Only if your personal experience and some miraculous events happen will people believe? Scripture holds a different view, when Jesus rebukes Thomas's disbelief because Thomas needed to touch and see the wounds.

---

8. Moreland, *Kingdom Triangle*, 179.
9. Moreland, *Kingdom Triangle*, 183.
10. Moreland, *Kingdom Triangle*, 183.

3

Objective Evidence

THE GOSPEL PROCLAIMED TO unbelievers and skeptics is the very Word of God. We have the message of salvation from sin, death, and the devil given to us through eyewitnesses. The evangelists wrote down what had actually occurred before their own eyes and in their hearing. The apostle Peter says to the Christians dispersed around the Roman Empire: "We did not follow cleverly devised myths when we made known to you the power and coming of our Lord Jesus Christ, but we were eyewitnesses" (2 Pet 1:16). The apostle Paul, when sharing what the gospel message is, reminds the Corinthian believers that what they believe was handed down to them, and there were over five hundred eyewitnesses (1 Cor 15:6). The apostle John goes into even greater detail when he writes,

> That which was from the beginning, which we have heard, which we have seen with our eyes, which we looked upon and have touched with our hands, concerning the word of life—the life was made manifest, and we have seen it, and testify to it and proclaim to you the eternal life, which was with the Father and was made manifest to us—that which we have seen and heard we proclaim also to you, so that you too may have fellowship with us. (1 John 1:1–3)

Objective Evidence

John states that the apostles heard, saw, and touched this Jesus who rose again. Over and over again, the apostles point to evidence as the reason for their authority to proclaim the risen Christ to others. They speak of themselves as eyewitnesses who touched, saw, and heard Jesus personally. They did not go by hearsay evidence but eyewitness testimony. As Craig Parton says regarding how to authenticate religious claims, "Verifiability is a critical component."[1] Without the ability to verify eyewitness testimony, the jury (those unbelievers and skeptics) may outright reject the gospel. The church has been graciously given this gift of an objective and verifiable message of good news to the world.

A Prima Facie Case

The legal term above simply means "at first view" or "on the first appearance." As a legal term, it holds that the evidence is true, valid, and sufficient to establish a fact or case, unless disproved. This is the type of evidence Christians have for the testimony of the evangelists (Matthew, Mark, Luke, and John) as well as the later testimony of the apostle Paul. The documentary evidence is so strong that unless the case can be disproved, it is to be accepted as true. What is being argued here is that their testimony, written in the Gospels and Acts, is true, and they saw with their own eyes the events recorded in them.

There are several tests to prove whether or not eyewitness testimony is true and valid, which I will go through briefly. First, is the eyewitness able to tell the truth? Is he or she willing to do so without much gain or loss? Are the eyewitnesses willing to suffer hardship or persecution? In the case of the New Testament writers, are they also willing to suffer a martyr's death? Can their reports be repudiated by others from their time, their own country, and people? In other words, are there adverse witnesses to their testimony? Then we look at the consistency in their testimonies. This does not mean they are absolutely identical, but rather, does their

---

1. Parton, *Religion on Trial*, 45.

combined testimony give us a consistent record for these events? Finally, we consider external corroboration through sources outside of the New Testament.

In courts of law, witnesses come forward for various reasons such as testifying and making known what happened. They affirm under oath that that which they testify is true. Often, witnesses provide evidence for their testimony, as in the case of St. Paul, who appeals to over five hundred eyewitnesses of the resurrected Jesus. He presents their testimony as evidence for the resurrection and that it should be believed. Eyewitnesses also bring in their personal knowledge in support of an asserted fact. In the absence of video testimony, a written statement may be given, and it holds the same weight as that which is recorded before the courts.

Who, then, are these eyewitnesses? The first and primary witness is Mary, Jesus's mother, who was first told would conceive a son while not having had relations with her espoused. She was then told that her cousin Elizabeth was with child, though no one else knew that yet, as given in the account by Luke. Matthew begins his account with the lineage of Jesus, which is a key component for Jewish believers who value a proper genealogy. Later, Papias would corroborate that Matthew wrote this gospel in his *Exposition of the Oracles of the Lord* (circa AD 125–40).

Next in order in the New Testament is the Gospel of Mark. In St. Peter's first epistle (1 Pet 5:13) we find that the apostle speaks of Mark's conversion to the faith. Tertullian remarks that Mark wrote the Gospel account under the direction of Peter, for which it was then given its authority as apostolic. Papias confirms this as well in his work noted above.

In the brother of Jesus named James, we have a fascinating testimony from his refusing to recognize Jesus as Messiah to his leading the church in Jerusalem. What happened to convince him that his half-brother was the Savior? The resurrection of Jesus is what convinces him, and he converts. When St. Paul appeals to eyewitnesses in 1 Cor 15:17, he marks out the apostles and James. Paul later speaks of seeing no other apostle "except James the Lord's brother" after his own conversion recorded in Acts 21:17–19.

Objective Evidence

The authority we have, as believers, is the written Word of God. As Christians defend the faith, using the very Word of God, they utilize the pattern modeled by the apostles themselves. The Word of God is a means of grace, that instrument which God ordained to be one way to give saving faith as well as to strengthen it. Evangelicals must utilize this gift of Word as they proclaim the gospel, and not their testimony or personal experiences. The Word of God is verifiable, not their personal *intra nos* feelings or understandings.

When Evangelicals use their personal opinions, feelings, or experiences, they have flat out given unbelievers a way out of believing the gospel. The unbeliever may now call into question everything the Christian is saying since he or she too has experiences, feelings, and opinions that are not based in objective facts. This bad theological approach to defending and proclaiming the faith mimics what false religions and cults have done through the centuries. Our sure footing remains upon the solid rock, the documentary evidence, and objective truths found only in the Word of God, which are the pillars of our faith (cf. 1 Tim 3:15).

Seven Sermons

Though there are over a dozen sermons to be read in the book of Acts, I have chosen seven from among them to show the pattern of the original apostles when proclaiming and defending the faith. These are taken from Peter, Stephen, John, and Paul. In reading, studying, and researching each of these sermons, a pattern was seen, which I will be emphasizing in each sermon. I encourage you to read along and recognize the pattern God gave to the church through the examples of the apostles and Stephen for both proclaiming and defending the Christian faith. Since the church is to proclaim Christ and him crucified and risen again, it behooves all believers, no matter their denomination or theological preferences, to follow the pattern set for us. We have been commissioned to "go into all the world" (cf. Matt 28:19–20) preaching the gospel, and to do so may require a change in focus back to an apostolic apologetic.

4

A Pattern Recovered

Recovering the Objective Truth for a Powerful Gospel Presentation

> Having reviewed the religious trends, we see clearly that true religion, which involves man's relation to a Supreme Being, must be guided by this Supreme Being, and this guidance must be tested by some standard outside of his emotional experience. In other words, if there is a God whom we worship and whom we serve, He must be above and beyond ourselves, and to prevent each one from thinking his own analytical mind or ecstatic emotion to be supreme. man must be given an objective standard outside of himself by which he may test his subjective spiritual emotions or his philosophies of life and thus protect him from erroneous concepts.[1]

EVERY BELIEVER MUST MOVE quickly from testifying of his or her own personal experience, away from his or her own denominational peculiarities, on to the gospel of Christ and him crucified and risen again. What then should a gospel defense and proclamation look like? Perhaps we do well to read and study the sermons found in the book of Acts and have the apostles teach

1. Christensen, "Subjective and Objective Religion (Concluded)."

A Pattern Recovered

us. In this chapter, what the apostles preached will be looked at. In total, ten of the sermons found in the book of Acts given by the original apostles and St. Paul will be utilized to see on what and whom the focus was in preaching and evangelizing. Do they focus on the ecstatic gifts, the miracles they did in the name of Jesus, or do they zero in on the verifiable resurrection of him from the dead? If the latter, then perhaps our Pentecostal and charismatic brothers and sisters will listen to the Word of God as their teacher and regain a robust evangel about the resurrection rather than their personal experiences or charismata.

Dr. Montgomery often refers to one purpose of apologetics as removing the hurdles on the road to the house of salvation. Keeping this analogy in mind, if we think of our personal testimony as the first stone on that cobble path, we never stay there when inviting others into our home. We walk off of that first stone and onto the next and so on until we read that door of salvation, on the outside of which its sign reads, "Whosoever will may enter." The path to that door is through the proclamation of the gospel—the life, death, and resurrection of Jesus based upon the truths the evangelists told us, which actually "occurred within their own personal knowledge"[2] and were recorded for us in verifiable eyewitness documentation.

Testimony may be a starting point, but our own experiences pale in verifiable comparison to the proofs God has given us in his Word. Testimony may get the conversation going, but believers must move quickly to the eyewitness accounts of the resurrection, because that is the culminating point of the gospel: forgiveness of sins, because Jesus rose again for our justification (Rom 4:25). Testimonies, no matter how dramatic, will not bring life and salvation. God has told us that life and salvation are given through Jesus Christ, who died and rose again for all people (Acts 4:12; Titus 2:11).

I grew up in a holiness Pentecostal church where feelings and experiences directed your life, and the emphasis on world missions was never a sideline. Christians of all walks of life were to be about working in the harvest field, going out into "all the world" (Matt

---

2. Greenleaf, "Testimony of the Evangelists."

28:19) to preach the gospel. However, the emphasis, as evidenced in this book, was focused more on the experiences the listeners could have, rather than on proclaiming Christ and him crucified and risen again. As Craig Parton writes, "Verifiability is a critical component when dealing with religious claims."[3] It is imperative, therefore, that Evangelicals and charismatics move from their personal experiences, which cannot be verified, to the resurrection, which is based upon verifiable predicates.[4]

It is with great love for my family and friends who still expect God to speak directly to them, with audible voice or through modern prophets and apostles, that this book has been presented. Far from diminishing the inward desire to proclaim Christ to the world, this has been who it is about: Jesus Christ and his life, death, and resurrection. The objective truth that the written Word of God has given usurps all subjective experiences and crushes the argument of feelings over facts. When the objective and verifiable truths of the gospel are proclaimed, apart from denomination and personal preferences, then it is truly the "power of God unto salvation" (Rom 1:16) as Scripture teaches us.

This subjective style of apologetics does nothing for a true gospel presentation and opens it up to rejection based on feelings and emotions. The modern idea that "what is true for you may not be true for me" relies upon subjectivism. However, the gospel is objectively true, and therefore what is true for me is most definitely true for you. This chapter will work on recovering the objective truth of the gospel so that we may present to others the facts of God's Word, apart from our feelings or emotional experiences. Through looking at the focus of the sermons from the book of Acts, it is the hope that those with a more subjective gospel which results in a feelings/experience-based proclamation will return to that which the apostles and early church declared: an objective truth which was validated by eyewitnesses given to the church in the Scriptures.

---

3. Parton, *Religion on Trial*, 45.
4. Parton, *Religion on Trial*, 55.

A Pattern Recovered

Bringing modern Evangelicals the tools needed to recover a true gospel presentation may even cause them to leave the Pentecostal model and join other churches that understand that God has spoken to us in his Son and that his Word is sufficient. It may help them to see that God works through objective truth, because his is the only real truth that matters. Feelings and emotions come and go, but God's Word stands forever.

Counter to popular opinion among many Evangelicals, Christianity is not based upon your experience, your feelings, or some direct message from God in your heart or mind. While Christianity does not reject that at times your feelings will swell with joy, it also teaches us that conviction of sin will bring down any euphoria quickly. Christianity based upon happy, joyful, exuberant emotions is not the Christianity of history nor of the Bible. There is no doubt that the individual may feel something in the Divine Service, after absolution or partaking of the true body and blood of Christ; but the faith is not based upon feelings but upon the object truth that God has said, "I forgive you of your sins."

God works from the outside first and then inwardly. However, Evangelicals have flipped the order which God has given in his Word and have made even the proclamation of the gospel one based upon whether it feels good. Luther reminded the church, which at that time was steeped in an inner focus for assurance of salvation, that God always works through the outward means (*extra nos*) first and then inwardly changes the person (*intra nos*).[5] That order is never to be confused, and yet the subjectivism of Pentecostalism has turned this order and the gospel completely upside down, with feet in the air and head in the sand.

It's Not about You

The presentation is of the gospel, not your particular denomination or theological system or your opinion, but about Jesus Christ who lived, died, was buried, and rose again, according to the

---

5. Luther, "Church and Ministry," 40.

Scriptures. For many of the Evangelicals with whom I grew up, apologetics seems quite unnecessary. Rather, we should just share what God has done for us and encourage people to make a decision. The idea for the Pentecostal is that by trying to defend the faith, we are replacing the work of the Holy Spirit. We are trying to use human reasoning to save people. In *Scaling the Secular City*, J. P. Moreland encourages even those within his charismatic circles to overcome their objections to using apologetics as one tool in the work of evangelism. He writes, "Apologetics is a ministry designed to help unbelievers over some intellectual obstacles and believers to remove doubts that hinder spiritual growth.[6]" He likens the use of apologetics to the use of the sermon in this vein. Further, he writes,

> Apologetics can help remove obstacles to faith and thus aid unbelievers in embracing the gospel. Certainly the Holy Spirit must be involved in drawing men to Christ. But a preacher is not absolved of the responsibility of preparing his sermon just because the Spirit must apply the Word of God to the lives of his listeners. In the same way, ambassadors for Christ are not excused from the responsibility of defending the gospel. The Spirit can use evidence to convict men of the truth of the proclamation.[7]

While the argument is that utilizing any argument or defense limits or replaces the work of the Holy Spirit, the Scriptures say differently. The apostle Peter states that when unbelievers or skeptics begin to question not only what we believe, we are to be prepared with an answer (*apologia*) and a defense of the faith. "Have no fear of them, nor be troubled, but in your hearts honor Christ the Lord as holy, always being prepared to make a defense to anyoe who asks you for a reason for the hope that is in you " (1 Pet 3:15). Notice how Peter reminds us that in preparing a reason for the hope we have—salvation in Christ from sin, death, and the devil—we "honor Christ." In no way do we supersede the work of the Holy Spirit with learning to defend the faith and then offering

---

6. Moreland, *Scaling the Secular City*, 11.
7. Moreland, *Scaling the Secular City*, 11.

that evidence to unbelievers. Rather, we actually do the work of an evangelist (2 Tim 4:5) just as we are told.

Experience simply cannot be the source of truth.[8] In the Corinthian church, which experienced many of the charismatic gifts, Paul closes his letter by reminding them "of the gospel I preached to you, which you received, in which you stand, and by which you are being saved" (1 Cor 15:1–2a). Recently, in a Bible study at the church I attend, Faith Lutheran, the following was shared regarding the purpose of the gifts of the Holy Spirit for the church:

> The spiritual gifts from the Spirit of Jesus flowed out of their relationship to Jesus as Savior and Lord—and were intended to be unifying facts, not divisive factors, in the life of the congregation. God gives spiritual gifts not to amaze and exalt the recipients but to equip them for service to the body.[9]

What is this gospel? Is the gospel about the gifts on which he just finished correcting them? No. The creedal statement by Paul is immediately used following his rebuke of how they were using the gifts. He refocuses their attention off the charismatic gifts and back on to the saving message of the gospel:

> For I delivered to you as of *first* importance what I also received: That Christ died for our sins in accordance with the Scripture, that he was buried, that he was raised on the third day in accordance with the Scriptures. (1 Cor 15:3; italics added)

Paul reminds the Corinthian church and every believer since that the gospel is not the gifts, the charismata, the experiences, or even the personal feelings the person may have. The cornerstone of the gospel is the resurrection, not personal feelings or opinions. As Professor Parton writes,

> Many claim truth through subjective religious experience espousing a "testimony" as an unchallengeable link to the

---

8. Parton, *Religion on Trial*, 29.
9. "Epistle for the Day."

truth. However, unfortunately, there are as many religious experiences and testimonies as there are religions.[10]

Paul had much to teach the Corinthians and the church, yet this is not what he reminds them as "first importance." He does not go into a diatribe about the gifts of the Spirit or Spirit baptism, except where he corrected them earlier in the letter; instead, reminds them of the gospel. What is that gospel? Jesus Christ died and rose again, according to the Scriptures. Paul is making the argument based upon the written Word of God. He does not tell them, remember how your heart warmed or a "burning of the bosom" took place when you heard? Remember the goose bumps you felt when the preacher called you forward to make a decision for the Lord? Remember how happy and gleeful you felt when the worship team began to play "Just as I Am"? Paul does not say that the proof of the resurrection was because Jesus lives in his heart. "You ask me how I know He lives? He lives within my heart," which we sing in many churches especially at Easter, is just bad theology. This is not proof. Nor is a "melody of love" proof that Jesus lived, died, was buried, and rose again, triumphing over death, hell, and the grave. In fact, the Mormons have a "burning bosom." How would you possibly argue against their feelings and subjective experiences as false? You cannot if you focus upon your own testimony. Subjective proof is not proof at all.

Instead, Paul immediately reminds the Corinthians of the objective truths of the life, death, and resurrection of Jesus. He points to evidence in the prophecies of the written Word of God. Paul then goes on to eyewitness accounts of the apostles, then to James the brother of Jesus who did not believe until the resurrection, and then to the five hundred eyewitnesses (others in the text) to show the objective proof of the resurrection. Paul does not appeal to their subjective experience; instead, he recalls the objective and verifiable facts of the death and resurrection of Jesus Christ for the sins of the world. Relying upon subjective testimony as a gospel presentation is validating every other religion in this world rather

---

10. Parton, *Religion on Trial*, 29.

A Pattern Recovered

than showing they are false, offer no hope, and bring only eternal damnation upon their believers. Christians have the Word of life and the words of life, if we but proclaim the Scriptures instead of our feelings.

The order of Paul's sermon is Jesus Christ's death and resurrection first. Paul appeals to the written Word first and foremost, then to the eyewitness testimonies of Peter, the other apostles, James and the others (a reference to the five hundred at the ascension?). Paul places himself, his experience on the road to Damascus, and his conversion at the end. His personal testimony is at the end of this reminder of the gospel. Paul is not central to it at all. Jesus is first, central, and the end, as Paul states that the resurrection is the central truth of the gospel.

Paul continues with the Corinthians' salvation being based upon these facts. If these reports, eyewitness testimony, and fulfillment of Scripture are wrong for declaring Jesus raised from the dead, then their belief is in vain. Paul does not argue from subjective experience. Rather, he argues from verifiable objective truth to prove that salvation from sin, death, and the devil is contingent upon Jesus's physical resurrection from the dead. Paul does not refer to speaking in tongues as verification of salvation. Paul does not preach subjective experiences but objective facts. If the resurrection did not occur, we all remain in our sins and should be pitied. This is the gospel which is, as Paul said to the Roman believers, "the power of God unto salvation" (Rom 1:16).

Let us review the pattern here:

> Christ's death is according to prophetic Scripture.
>
> Christ's resurrection is according to prophetic Scripture.
>
> Eyewitnesses testify of Christ's physical death and resurrection for the forgiveness of our sins.

In each of the sermons looked at in the remaining part of this chapter, it will be noted that the appeal is to prophetic scriptures and verified by eyewitness testimony(ies). If we are to learn how to proclaim and defend the faith, we would do well to follow the pattern set forth in Scripture. This pattern relies upon objective events and not subjective feelings or experiences.

How Did the Apostles in Acts Proclaim the Gospel?

When I was growing up in a holiness-Pentecostal church, formal study of the Scriptures was not encouraged. It was taught that since we were Spirit-baptized and have the Bible, that was all we needed to go out and tell others about Jesus. No professors or seminary training were needed. If you did feel that you needed training, then two options were offered: Pentecostal Bible school or, in our denomination, life in a "Faith Home" to be trained. Still, formal education in smaller Pentecostal churches is not strongly encouraged, since seminaries are the spiritual equivalent of cemeteries. In light of this, I have decided, in presenting an apologetic to my Pentecostal and charismatic brothers and sisters, to present what the apostles proclaimed as gospel, in the hopes that they too will begin to put aside their own experiences and theological predilections for a truly biblical one.

In the Acts of the Apostles there are well over fifteen sermons. Of that abundance there are ten which are gospel presentations to Jews, Gentile believers (converts to Judaism), and pagan Gentiles, which will enable us to see what the core message is in proclaiming and defending the Christian faith. From those ten, I have selected seven to review. Learning from Peter, Stephen, and Paul will equip us with a proper apologetic/proclamation style and one that truly mirrors theirs.

Eyewitness Testimony

In the church in which I grew up and the charismatic fellowships I served and attended, I learned to tell others about Jesus. While the focus was more about the gifts than the Giver, nevertheless, the passion to witness was fed, and only when I was a staunch Calvinist did that become less important. However, it was after

A Pattern Recovered

my conversion to Lutheranism that the smoldering twigs that remained were fanned to become a steady burning fire. The love and passion I had to evangelize and defend the faith has burned brightly, and it is the purpose for this presentation. Although I grew up Pentecostal, where education in theology, philosophy, and such things were not greatly encouraged, God providentially overruled that thinking and directed my steps in the direction of apologetics for my degrees. However, I have not lost sight of the fact that it is Christ we are proclaiming, and the best source we have to aid us in that presentation is the Scriptures. Through lessons learned via Dr. Montgomery and Trinity Seminary, the position of logical reasoning and historical and documentary evidence was never placed above the written Word of God.

Therefore, the apologetic I am offering to my brothers and sisters in the Pentecostal and charismatic world is the pattern found in the Scriptures. It is an apostolic apologetic if there ever was one. Utilizing the sermons of the book of Acts from the evangelists, along with the epistles from the apostles, it is my desire that the reader will find the biblical pattern which indeed is the judicial and evidential apologetic that Dr. Montgomery has taught for decades. Far from placing human reasoning above the Scriptures, this pattern will give you the tools you need to defend the faith. These tools will bring you back from a subjective, personal testimony-focused approach to that which the apostles used.

Objective Proclamation of the Gospel

Objective truth demands objective proclamation and defense. The apostles and evangelists of the four Gospels and the book of Acts present to us a pattern to follow, which St. Paul gives us in 1 Cor 15: Jesus died, was buried, and rose again, according to the Scriptures. Paul then tells the order of Jesus's physical appearances to his disciples, first Peter, then James, the five hundred, and lastly to Paul. They are the eyewitnesses of these things, not contemporary Christians. The message is to be one that brings out the objective truths found in the documentary evidence of Matthew, Mark,

They Were Eyewitnesses

Luke, John and the Acts of the Apostles. This is the pattern we are to follow because it is the one the Scriptures give. Contemporary Christians of every theological style needs to move away from the subjective "I feel it's true because" style and back to presenting the gospel the way the apostles did. Again, *they were eyewitnesses,* not you or me.

5

Peter Sets the Pattern

Peter's Sermon at Pentecost:
Sermon #1: **Acts 2:14–21**

> But Peter, standing with the eleven, lifted up his voice and addressed them: "Men of Judea and all who dwell in Jerusalem, let this be known to you, and give ear to my words. For these people are not drunk, as you suppose, since it is only the third hour of the day. But this is what was uttered through the prophet Joel:
>> "'And in the last days it shall be, God declares,
>> that I will pour out my Spirit on all flesh,
>> and your sons and your daughters shall prophesy,
>> and your young men shall see visions,
>> and your old men shall dream dreams;
>> even on my male servants and female servants
>> in those days I will pour out my Spirit, and they shall prophesy.
>> And I will show wonders in the heavens above
>> and signs on the earth below,
>> blood, and fire, and vapor of smoke;
>> the sun shall be turned to darkness
>> and the moon to blood,
>> before the day of the Lord comes, the great and magnificent day.

They Were Eyewitnesses

And it shall come to pass that everyone who calls upon the name of the Lord shall be saved.'

"Men of Israel, hear these words: Jesus of Nazareth, a man attested to you by God with mighty works and wonders and signs that God did through him in your midst, as you yourselves know—this Jesus, delivered up according to the definite plan and foreknowledge of God, you crucified and killed by the hands of lawless men. God raised him up, loosing the pangs of death, because it was not possible for him to be held by it."

THIS PASSAGE IS VERY familiar to Christians worldwide. It is the birth of the church as we know it. There is no denying that God's people existed as the nation of Israel and yet now, on this first Pentecost, God is publishing the good news globally and inviting Gentiles to come en masse. There is no difference between the people of God in Moses, the Psalms, and the Prophets (often called the Old Testament) and the people of God now, except that Israel was before the incarnation, death, burial, and resurrection of Jesus, and we come after that. Two sides of the same people, with Jesus joining us hand in hand. Christians are, after all, as the Scriptures says, "of the faith of Abraham" (see Rom 4:1–3) and were grafted into the one true faith. This is the first sermon from Peter on the day the Holy Spirit was poured out on the apostles and those in the upper room that Sunday morning.

Peter is boldly explaining to the crowd that what they are witnessing is a fulfillment of the Scriptures. Peter declares that they are seeing Joel 2 fulfilled right before their eyes. Note how Peter refers to the eleven who were eyewitnesses of the events during Passover when the leaders arrested, crucified, and buried Jesus. Peter immediate moves from this fulfillment of prophecy, which is proof that what they were seeing was God's work, to the cross and resurrection.

Nowhere does Peter tell them all about tongues and visions as the core of what is happening. Instead, Peter uses the event of which they are eyewitnesses to validate that they are eyewitnesses of Jesus's resurrection. Peter's appeal is a legal one: eyewitness testimony. He uses the crowd's eyewitnessing of these events and also

Peter Sets the Pattern

speaks immediately to Jesus. Peter reminds them that Jesus was validated as to who he is by God through the miracles and signs that were done. He tells the people "you were there," when he says "God did through him in your midst, as you yourselves know." Peter is referencing the eyewitness accounts to which those in the crowd of onlookers could testify. Peter does not go into the charismatic experiences of the apostles and disciples of Jesus who were in the upper room, except to state the event as fulfillment of Joel's Old Testament prophecy. Peter's speaking authoritatively was based not upon his experience but rather upon the authority of the prophets.

> Nothing is more forceful than to argue with them (skeptics) from prophecy, which was even more forceful than facts.[1]

Peter in his second letter reaffirms prophetic fulfillment and the Scriptures as a better and more reliable test than even his experiences on the Mount of Transfiguration when he writes,

> For we did not follow cleverly devised myths when we made known to you the power and coming of our Lord Jesus Christ, but we were *eyewitnesses of his majesty*. For when he received honor and glory from God the Father, and the voice was borne to him by the Majestic Glory, "This is my beloved Son, with whom I am well pleased," we ourselves heard this very voice born from heaven, for we were with him on the holy mountain. *And we have something more sure, the prophetic word*, to which *you will do well to pay attention* as to a lamp shining in a dark place, until the day dawns and the morning star rises in your hearts, know this first of all, that *no prophecy of Scripture comes from someone's own interpretation*. (2 Pet 1:16–20; italics added)

Peter is arguing from fulfilled Scripture and prophecy. As Chrysostom reiterates, nothing is more forceful than arguing from facts, eyewitness testimony, and from the Scriptures themselves in fulfilled prophecies. Further, when Christ performed miracles, many rejected him. However, when Jesus quoted fulfilled prophecy,

---

1. Chrysostom, quoted in Martin and Oden, *Acts*, 28.

the people could not dispute him. Peter is doing the same thing: arguing from the Scriptures. Peter does not base his argument on his own experiences, either on the Mount of Transfiguration or of Pentecost. Rather, Peter argues from the power of God's own written Word.

Immediately after quoting the fulfillment of Joel's prophecy, right before their very eyes, he moves to the gospel. Peter does not remain on what had been or was being seen and experienced but rather jumps off the testimonial point right into what was crucial to the hearers. We do well to take notice of how quickly Peter does this and copy his form, moving from our own personal testimony to that which truly saves: the gospel.

In fact, Peter links what they are seeing on this Pentecost (the fulfillment of Joel) right to the resurrection. That Jesus is risen as prophesied in Ps 15 and now is in a position of authority as foretold in Ps 110, Peter says that this is verified by the fact of the outpouring of the Spirit. Peter's focus is no longer on the strange tongues the audience heard (which were true earthly languages) but on how that pouring out of the Holy Spirit proves the resurrection happened.

The very next thing Peter does is to remind the listeners that they crucified this Lord of glory. With "lawless hands" they nailed the Son of God to a cross and killed him. Peter brings in the law of God when he reminds them that murdering an innocent is breaking God's commandments, and they are every bit as guilty as the rulers in the Sanhedrin. Peter's use of the law is short and bitter, but he does not leave them there. Peter had already given them the antidote to their sin problem when he said, "Everyone who calls upon the name of the Lord shall be saved" (v. 21). Peter reminds them that the resurrection of Christ was because death had no right to him and could not hold or contain him. This is the gospel: Jesus died and rose again so that we sinners may be saved.

Peter's focus in this very first sermon of the church is not on the gifts or the tongues of fire or the experiences of the apostles and disciples gathered in the upper room on that Pentecost. Nor is his focus on the audience's witness of this phenomena and their amazement. The focus of Peter's sermon is twofold: fulfillment of Scripture and the gospel of Christ, who died and rose again for their salvation.

Too often at the church in which I grew up and that I attended after my conversion, the focus was upon the charismata, the experiences one could have through Spirit-baptism. Too often the sermons preached even to the congregation were about the charismatic gifts one could have to live victoriously. The focus was on subjective experiences for today rather than on the objective facts of fulfilled Scripture and the gospel. What if I did not have those experiences? Was I any less of a Christian because I lacked a "personal Pentecost"? How often I went down to the altar to repent and beg God for these subjective experiences rather than bask in the forgiveness of my sins! When the focus is not upon an event that happened two thousand years ago, which fulfilled Scripture in verifying the resurrection, then one ends up with a distorted gospel message to tell others. Peter reminds us in his first sermon to use the fulfillment of Scriptures and proclaim the gospel so that they may believe and be saved.

6

Following the Apostles

Sermon #2: **Acts 3:12–26**

> While he clung to Peter and John, all the people, utterly astounded, ran together to them in the portico called Solomon's. And when Peter saw it he addressed the people: "Men of Israel, why do you wonder at this, or why do you stare at us, as though by our own power or piety we have made him walk? The God of Abraham, the God of Isaac, and the God of Jacob, the God of our fathers, glorified his servant Jesus, whom you delivered over and denied in the presence of Pilate, when he had decided to release him. But you denied the Holy and Righteous One, and asked for a murderer to be granted to you, and you killed the Author of life, whom God raised from the dead. To this we are witnesses. And his name—by faith in his name—has made this man strong whom you see and know, and the faith that is through Jesus has given the man this perfect health in the presence of you all.
>
> "And now, brothers, I know that you acted in ignorance, as did also your rulers. But what God foretold by the mouth of all the prophets, that his Christ would suffer, he thus fulfilled. Repent therefore, and turn back, that your sins may be blotted out, that times of refreshing may come from the presence of the Lord, and that

Following the Apostles

he may send the Christ appointed for you, Jesus, whom heaven must receive until the time for restoring all the things about which God spoke by the mouth of his holy prophets long ago. Moses said, 'The Lord God will raise up for you a prophet like me from your brothers. You shall listen to him in whatever he tells you. And it shall be that every soul who does not listen to that prophet shall be destroyed from the people.' And all the prophets who have spoken, from Samuel and those who came after him, also proclaimed these days. You are the sons of the prophets and of the covenant that God made with your fathers, saying to Abraham, 'And in your offspring shall all the families of the earth be blessed.' God, having raised up his servant, sent him to you first, to bless you by turning every one of you from your wickedness."

THIS INTERACTION OF PETER and John with the cripple at the temple is often referred to by Evangelicals as proof that believers should be working the miraculous. As Scripture shows, the prophets of old, when being authenticated as true prophets of God, performed miracles. (Actually, they did not do them, but God did them through them.) In the same way, God was authenticating the apostles as New Testament prophets of God, proclaiming the good news and validating their message through miracles. As Rev. Walter Chantry states, "New Testament miracles serve precisely the same end as those of the old covenant . . . .They were calling attention to the Divine authority of his (Jesus') teaching . . . and to the Apostles as spokesmen of God's infallible Word."[1]

Let's look closer at what this sermon teaches believers about gospel proclamation and the defense of the faith. First, this is an amazing miracle, and the people around begin to run to Peter and John. Peter sees this and does what? He immediately talks to them about the healing gifts, that if they simply believe, they too can receive them—right? No. Okay, so they begin to call many up and blow on them and slay them in the spirit? No. Well, they tell them about Pentecost and how God is restoring the gifts of the Spirit, and they too can heal and deliver people from sickness, right? That

---

1. Chantry, *Signs of the Apostles*, 12, 15.

would be a resounding no. The apostles speak of Jesus's death, burial, and resurrection. In this sermon, we find Peter not speaking of his personal experience but what he witnessed with his own eyes and ears.

Just as when Pentecost happened and it fulfilled the prophecy of Joel in order to show that the Jesus they crucified was risen from the dead and poured out his Spirit because he has all authority, so too Peter references the Old Testament, the prophets, and the resurrection of Jesus. Peter does not get into tertiary theology but remains firmly planted on the death and resurrection of Jesus Christ. The apostle Peter immediately moves from the verifiable miracle to the verifiable cross and resurrection of Jesus. These people physically saw this man healed, and though that is why they rushed forward, Peter is not about to remain on the topic of miracles. He didn't remain on the topic of tongues in the first sermon (Acts 2), and he won't here either.

Watch the objective gospel go out through Peter's proclamation when he says, "You denied the Holy and Righteous One." There is not a doubt that people at the portico of Solomon were citizens of Jerusalem, and while they may not have been among the crowd that chanted "crucify him," they knew what had happened. How do we know this? Peter tells them you "asked for a murderer to be granted to you, and you killed the Author of life." Peter gives them the law again. He charges them with complicity in the murder of the Author of life. He appeals to them being eyewitnesses of the trial and brutal execution of Jesus when Pilate wanted to release him. They, says Peter, were eyewitnesses of this.

In the same way, Peter proclaims the resurrection of Jesus. He goes on to say (v. 15b), "whom God raised from the dead. To this we are witnesses." Just as these Jews were eyewitnesses of the facts of the trial, crucifixion, execution, and death of Jesus, Peter declares, "We are witnesses." Peter does not appeal to their emotions at the sight of a healed man, nor even to the healed man. He appeals to the prophets of old and to eyewitness testimony.

Not one of us reading this book was an eyewitness of these events, but the testimony we have is by the evangelists and apostles who were actually living when all of this occurred. The four Gospels and the book of Acts record the events by those who actually witnessed them. Strangely they do not tell us about subjective feelings, thoughts, or their opinions. They are the witnesses to these events, not us. We know of the events because they have been authenticated as true and verifiable eyewitness accounts. Peter says this: "We are witnesses." If the listeners you gather around want to refute anything, they must bring forth verifiable proof that the apostles were not true eyewitnesses and the events of which they tell us did not actually occur. What makes us think that our stories are better than the historical, documented, verifiable testimony of these eyewitnesses? God's Word has not said our "stories are the power of salvation" but rather his gospel is.

In fact, the miracle "points out how sure the apostles were of Jesus' resurrection since they attribute the miracle to him." Peter argues from the miracle to the resurrection of Jesus and then proclaims the gospel. His argument is that what God said in his written Word by the mouths of the prophets is proven by the resurrection.

Peter does not speak of the miracle of the lame man walking, except as proof that Jesus rose from the dead. He also does not point to himself, because that might raise "too high a notion of himself."[2] It's as if Peter is saying, "Do *not* look at us." This is very different from the Pentecostal and charismatic meetings I would attend, where the speaker's name was in lights and everyone just wanted to be touched by him or her or receive a "word from God" for them. The man or woman was the focus, the miracle worker, the seer or prophet of God, rather than the gospel. Peter and the other apostles, all eyewitnesses of the resurrected Jesus, did not put their names on placards or billboards. They did not exalt the miracle. In fact, they usually jumped right off that point within moments and onto the resurrection of Jesus as foretold by the prophets of old. It behooves believers, no matter their denomination, to do the same. Don't stay on your testimony but on that of the evangelists and apostles, because *they were eyewitnesses.*

---

2. Chrysostom, quoted in Martin and Oden, *Acts,* 38.

They Were Eyewitnesses

If you argue that the miracle validates a person's ministry, perhaps this quote from the ancient church will help correct that:

> For often, as was said, people of corrupt minds, reprobates concerning the truth, both cast out devils and performed the greatest miracles in the name of the Lord.[3]

Or perhaps you prefer the words of Jesus:

> Not everyone who says to me, "Lord, Lord," will enter the kingdom of heaven, but the one who does the will of my Father who is in heaven. On that day many will say to me, "Lord, Lord, did we not prophesy in your name, and cast out demons in your name, and do many mighty works in your name?" And then will I declare to them, "I never knew you; depart from me, you workers of lawlessness." (Matt 7:21–23)

Instead of piling praise onto themselves, Peter and John immediately point to Jesus and his resurrection. They themselves confess that it was not by their own power but by that of Christ. If these two evangelists/apostles did not truly believe that Christ had risen again, they would not have been willing to establish the honor of a dead man rather than their own.[4] However, they emphasize that this miracle was done in the name of Jesus, because God raised him from the dead, and that faith is given through Jesus.

Follow the pattern set out by the apostles:

Testimony:

The lame man walks and witnesses are astounded.

Proclamation:

Christ, whom you killed ...

The prophets spoke of Jesus.

They were eyewitnesses of the execution of Jesus.

---

3. John Cassian, quoted in Martin and Oden, *Acts*, 40.
4. Schaff, ed., *Select Library*, 11:58.

> Some cried out "crucify him" when Pilate wanted to release Jesus.
>
> Jesus is risen from the dead: God raised him up from the dead.
>
> Repent and be forgiven:
>
> God having raised up his servant sent him to you first to bless you by turning every one of you from your wickedness. (v. 26)

Note the pattern Peter again uses. While testimony can be a starting point, Peter immediately jumps off of it and onto the Scriptures. Peter says the miracle only proves that this Jesus, in whose name the lame man was healed, has risen from the dead and is the Author of life. The resurrection is proof that God is calling all people to repent of their sins and be forgiven. This is the gospel.

The same way the first evangelists and the apostles proclaimed and defended the gospel is the pattern we are to use today. Christians are to be proclaiming Christ crucified, died, and risen, and not our particular theological persuasion nor our own personal experiences. Gospel proclamation must be objective, because it is only the objective verifiable truth that saves.

Let us remember the pattern which Paul said was passed down (received), evidently from the first apostles: that Christ died for our sins in accordance with the Scriptures, that he was buried, that he was raised on the third day in accordance with the Scriptures (1 Cor 15:3–4)

7

Proclaiming the Name of Jesus

Sermon #3: **Peter's Defense in Acts 4:5-12**

> On the next day their rulers and elders and scribes gathered together in Jerusalem, with Annas the high priest and Caiaphas and John and Alexander, and all who were of the high-priestly family. And when they had set them in the midst, they inquired, "By what power or by what name did you do this?" Then Peter, filled with the Holy Spirit, said to them, "Rulers of the people and elders, if we are being examined today concerning a good deed done to a crippled man, by what means this man has been healed, let it be known to all of you and to all the people of Israel that by the name of Jesus Christ of Nazareth, whom you crucified, whom God raised from the dead—by him this man is standing before you well. This Jesus is the stone that was rejected by you, the builders, which has become the cornerstone. And there is salvation in no one else, for there is no other name under heaven given among men by which we must be saved."

THE APOSTLE PETER BEGINS his defense, his apologetic, with the objective truth. He starts the defense with a verifiable miracle of that to which many were actual eyewitnesses. He does not begin with his personal testimony or subjective experience. He does not begin with himself. Instead, Peter begins with Jesus healing this man before countless onlookers. They saw this and then heard Peter preach in the name of Jesus, which is what got the apostles hauled before the rulers, elders, and high priest.

Peter challenges them with the facts that a man was healed; a cripple now walks. Evidence is clear. Peter knows they can see this for themselves. As Paul would later say, it did not "happen in a corner" (Acts 26:26). Peter then launches into the gospel: this Jesus you crucified, God raised from the dead (v. 11). The pattern for both proclamation and defense of the faith is the gospel, not a subjective experience or feeling. Peter proclaims Jesus Christ crucified, died, and risen again. Peter states that because Jesus is alive, this cripple walks. The miracle itself is authenticating the resurrection of Jesus and his authority over all things. Peter immediately moves from the miracles/experience to the gospel as verified by the Old Testament prophets.

Then, the apostle presents the prophets of old to the leaders, showing proof from the written Word that God raised Jesus from the dead. The appeal, once again, is not towards Peter's own incredible experiences with Jesus. He does not talk about his "mountaintop experience" (cf. 2 Pet 1:16–20) but instead brings in the Scriptures, the prophecies fulfilled by Jesus which pointed to his resurrection, as his authority for proclaiming the gospel. Peter rejects subjective presentation for an objective proclamation of the verifiable miracle of this cripple, which authenticates the resurrection of Jesus.

Read what Peter is proclaiming: "Let it be known to all of you and to all the people of Israel that by the name of Jesus Christ of Nazareth, whom you crucified, whom God raised from the dead— by him this man is standing before you well" (v. 10). The point of Peter's defense and apologetics is the resurrection of Jesus Christ. He reminds the people that they crucified Jesus, and God raised him from the dead. These were undisputed facts. Our Lord had gone before these rulers, and they handed him over to Pilate and roused the crowd to crucify him and release Barabbas. These same rulers had the tomb sealed and a Roman guard placed so that no one would steal the body. Then, these same rulers paid the guards to not report the resurrection. These same rulers and priests knew the Scriptures of old, and as Bede says, "They found in the prophetic Scripture Christ,"[1] and proceeded to reject him who is the chief cornerstone (v.11: "This Jesus is the stone that was rejected by you, the builders, which has become the cornerstone").

Following the pattern set from the beginning at Pentecost, Peter moves from the objective truths of the death and resurrection of Jesus, verified by this miracle that could not be disputed, to the call to believe and repent. Peter's gospel defense and apologetic is the death and physical resurrection of Jesus into the call to believe. His call is not to remind them of a subjective experience but a verifiable miracle done in the name of Jesus, and under his authority he calls men everywhere to repent. Peter consistently refers to the prophecies fulfilled in proclaiming the resurrection of Jesus.

The early church had the Scriptures, the Old Testament which testified about Jesus. This was their objective standard and must be ours as well. It is not denied that each apostle had a personal testimony, a subjective experience with the risen Christ, but that was not the apostles' focus nor motivation. What motivated them all was the resurrection of Jesus. This was the impetus behind their preaching, teaching, and defending the faith so much that most of them died a martyr's death for what they had eyewitnessed. Although they had their own subjective experience, they had the Scripture, which guided them in interpreting their personal experiences. Today, it seems we elevate experiences above the objective truths of the written Word of God. The apostles had to have something outside of themselves to give guidance to their subjective experience.[2]

---

1. Bede, quoted in Martin and Oden, *Acts,* 40.
2. Christensen, "Subjective and Objective Religion."

8

Deathbed Testimony

I WROTE AT THE beginning of this book that deathbed testimony is the most powerful in a courtroom. Why? People tell the truth when they know they are going to die. Here, in Acts 7, is the first deathbed testimony of an eyewitness. Stephen, a deacon, one of the seven chosen to serve the people in Jerusalem, has proclaimed Jesus as true Messiah risen from the dead, and he is in serious trouble for his eyewitness testimony. In the face of a horrific death by stoning, Stephen does not back down. He knows what he has seen and heard. He knows through personal experience and knowledge that Jesus is alive, having conquered sin, death, and the devil, and he will continue preaching right up to the point of death. Stephen declares with boldness that Jesus is seated at the right hand of God the Father Almighty and compassionately prays that God will forgive these doubters for the sin of murdering him simply because he proclaimed Jesus. Let us read what he proclaims and see that he, too, follows the pattern of the other apostles.

Sermon #4: A Deacon's Sermon (Acts 7)

Stephen's apologetic and proclamation follows the same pattern as set by Peter's sermons which have been reviewed. Stephen argues from the Scriptures that Jesus is the One promised to Israel and the world. His argument builds upon each of the historical records from Abraham to Moses. He continues to refer to the Scriptures, the prophets of old, and the promises of God. Finally, in vv. 51–53, Stephen concludes and summarizes all these prophecies as fulfilled in Jesus Christ:

> You stiff-necked people, uncircumcised in heart and ears, you always resist the Holy Spirit. As your fathers did, so do you. Which of the prophets did your fathers not persecute? And they killed those who announced beforehand the coming of the Righteous One, whom you have now betrayed and murdered, you who received the law as delivered by angels and did not keep it.

At this point, the people are so cut to the heart they become angry and pick up stones to murder Stephen. Then, Stephen gives eyewitness testimony to the risen Savior when he says, "Behold, I see the heavens opened, and the Son of Man standing at the right hand of God." Stephen's objective testimony is that he sees Jesus, the Son of Man, at the right hand of God, where all authority is given. He pleads with God, as did his risen Lord, that this sin not be held against them.

Once again we have a pattern in the book of Acts from the apostles and the early church which needs to be followed. Traditionally, at any revival or meeting I attended within the Pentecostal or charismatic church, the pattern was as follows: share your testimony, which usually included how horrific a sinner you were. Often, on Sunday nights at church, when testimony time came, there seemed to be a rush as to who could share the most degrading sins they once committed and how now they were "living for Jesus." I remember often doing the same and not focusing upon the death and resurrection of Jesus as the reason my sins were forgiven.

Deathbed Testimony

At revival or miracle meetings and conferences, the message tended to focus on the miraculous or visions and dreams instead of on the saving power of God in Christ because of His life, death, and resurrection. There would be "testimony time," where individuals stood to tell of their personal conversions to Christianity and their experiences. Many would bring unsaved friends and family, because they thought that if they heard about the miraculous or of some exciting and dramatic conversion story, they would be convinced and turn to Christ. The unbeliever would then be encouraged to come forward and "make a decision for Jesus," the emphasis being on receiving this "power" to live for God and to do the miraculous.

But this is all backwards and just wrong if we want to follow the biblical pattern for evangelism and apologetics. We do not talk about ourselves, our experiences, our personal conversion. Instead, the pattern laid out in the Scripture is to talk about Jesus: His life, death, burial, and resurrection in accord with the accounts by the evangelists and apostles. God tells us in his Word that the power for salvation is the gospel (Rom 1:16–17), not our personal testimony. God tells us that it is through the foolishness of preaching (proclaiming Christ) that he brings about conversion. The apostle Paul warns that the Jews demand signs (similar to modern charismatics demanding signs and wonders) and the Greeks seek wisdom (philosophical arguments), but both are stumbling blocks and hindrances. Instead, St. Paul says, "We preach Christ . . . for the foolishness of God is wiser than men, and the weakness of God is stronger than men." What is this folly? It is that God himself became a little baby, who grew up and lived a life of perfect obedience to the law, died in our place, was buried, and literally rose again so that all who believe this message, not your personal testimony, will be saved. This is the correct pattern, and Christians would be wise to follow what God ordained as the pattern for proclamation.

If you think you need to add miracles, philosophical arguments, or your personal testimony/experiences to enhance the gospel presentation or to make it more palatable, then you are saying that "mere Christianity" is not enough to convince the world of the truth and verifiability of the gospel based upon the Word of God alone. In fact, the writers of the *Formula of Concord* (part of the confessional Lutheran standards) write that Luther "always warned against using [philosophical terms] . . . such terms provided great potential for needless offense, confusion, and misunderstanding."[1] The question with this type of perspective is then this: is the gospel proclamation not enough? Scripture rejects this quite plainly when it says "the gospel is the power of God unto salvation" (Rom 1:16); "what we proclaim is not ourselves, but Jesus Christ as Lord" (2 Cor 4:5); and "the word of the cross is folly to those who are perishing, but to us who are being saved it is the power of God" (1 Cor 1:21–25).

Through the foolishness of preaching, God has chosen to save men and women of all ages throughout the world. He did not say that the power of God lay in your testimony or your personal experience but in the gospel (death, burial, and resurrection of Jesus). The reason for this is that you can be refuted. Your own experience, while it may be a starting point in talking with an unbeliever, can never give them life. You must bring them the Word of life, Jesus, through the gospel. God saves through the preaching of his written Word, the gospel of Jesus Christ. If "mere Christianity" is not enough, then all the promises of God, that it is through hearing the Word and receiving the sacraments that faith is granted, are false. If the gospel is not the power of God, then you make God a liar. If his Word is not sufficient, then you might as well not preach it. However, God is not a liar, and his promises are yes and amen (2 Cor 1:15). How did people ever come to true faith in Christ? Scripture says they came to true faith through the preaching and teaching of "mere Christianity," through Word and sacrament.

---

1. McCain, *Concordia*, 471.

9

The One Who Died and Now Lives Gives Life

Sermon #5: **Peter's Sermon to Believing Gentiles (Acts 10:36–43)**

THIS SERMON PROCLAIMS TO us that the One who was once dead is very much alive, having risen from the dead. This One now gives life to all who are dead in their sins and trespasses. Simply put, the One (Jesus) who was dead and now is alive gives life to those now dead in sin. Isn't that what proclaiming and defending the faith is all about? Telling those dead in sins that Jesus offers the forgiveness of sins and life everlasting? This is the message we too, Christians two millennia away from the historic events, are to proclaim, just like the apostles and evangelists did. We contemporary believers are to proclaim the ancient message, because it is there that the Holy Spirit works true faith and grants eternal life.

> As for the word that he sent to Israel, preaching good news of peace through Jesus Christ (he is Lord of all), you yourselves know what happened throughout all Judea, beginning from Galilee after the baptism that John proclaimed: how God anointed Jesus of Nazareth with the Holy Spirit and with power. He went about doing

good and healing all who were oppressed by the devil, for God was with him. And we are witnesses of all that he did both in the country of the Jews and in Jerusalem. They put him to death by hanging him on a tree, but God raised him on the third day and made him to appear, not to all the people but to us who had been chosen by God as witnesses, who ate and drank with him after he rose from the dead. And he commanded us to preach to the people and to testify that he is the one appointed by God to be judge of the living and the dead. To him all the prophets bear witness that everyone who believes in him receives forgiveness of sins through his name.

Another familiar sermon and text for modern Evangelicals is Peter's sermon to gentile believers in Cornelius's house. Many modern Evangelicals, charismatics, and Pentecostals focus on the charismata gifts received while missing the whole point of the sermon. They incorrectly think that this sermon of St. Peter proves that the Pentecostal charismatic gifts are given to every believer in all places and times. However, what Peter came to understand, via the vision of the sheet with food on it, was that the gospel is for everyone, Jew and gentile alike.

A closer examination of this sermon sees that the focus is not on the gifts but on the Giver of life, Jesus Christ. Peter begins by stating several objective facts with which even Cornelius and his household were familiar. Peter states, "You yourselves know what happened," and brings in the baptism of Jesus and the anointing of Jesus there, his teachings and "doing good and healing," because God was with him. God is teaching Peter that his vision of various unclean foods (Acts 10:9–16) is really about the gospel of Jesus going to the gentiles as well. This good news is not just for the Jewish nation but for people around the world. Peter, when he begins to preach to Cornelius's household, talks about God's impartiality. After that opening, Peter then proclaims the gospel, the true gift of God, not the charismatic gifts.

Peter then confirms that they are eyewitnesses: "And we are witnesses of all that he did" (v. 39) and saw all that Jesus did. He gives eyewitness, objective testimony that Jesus was executed on

The One Who Died and Now Lives Gives Life

the cross, and that God then raised Him from the dead. Further, he recounts that the apostles actually ate and drank with Jesus after the resurrection, validating that Jesus was neither a phantom nor a ghost but physically alive. Theodoret of Cyr says, "For since eating is proper to them that live, this present life, of necessity the Lord by means of eating and drinking proved the resurrection of the flesh to those who did not acknowledge it be real."[1] This is Peter's firsthand eyewitness testimony to the truth. Once again we do not see Peter retelling his personal experience on the Mount of Transfiguration nor even about how after his confession of faith Jesus rebuked him for not liking the idea of Jesus's death. In fact, Peter does not recount to Cornelius his experience of speaking in another language or of fire sitting on him. Instead, Peter gives his eyewitness testimony to Jesus's death and resurrection.

About what was Peter to testify? "He commanded us to preach to the people, and to testify that he is the one ordained to be judge of the living and the dead" (v. 42). Further, Peter then brings in the prophets of old. He says, "To him all the prophets bear witness" (v. 43). Peter once again does not rely upon subjective inward experience but testifies to objective proof. Then, having based his proclamation on the resurrection of Jesus, Peter proclaims that anyone and everyone who believes in Jesus "receives forgiveness of sins through his name" (v. 43). This pattern is repeated over and over in the Acts of the Apostles.

This historical event, recorded for us by St. Luke, shines on the truth that some people are seeking to live for God but do not have all the facts about Jesus. Peter informs Cornelius of the whole story of Jesus; Cornelius, then having a full and complete comprehension of the truth, believes and is saved.[2] Access to this salvation, as Gregory of Nyssa writes, comes through his (Jesus's) sin-and-death-destroying incarnation, crucifixion, death, and resurrection in which our souls participate through faith in Christ, the anointed One.[3]

---

1. Theodoret of Cyr, quoted in Martin and Oden, *Acts*, 133.
2. See Irenaeus in Martin and Oden, *Acts*, 133.
3. Gregory of Nyssa, quoted in Martin and Oden, *Acts*, 134.

They Were Eyewitnesses

Many in our contemporary society, just like Cornelius, have some knowledge of Jesus but don't know Jesus. Therefore, Peter gives Cornelius more information than Cornelius may have heard about the man of Nazareth. Peter explains how Jesus performed miracles, delivering all who were oppressed by the devil and proclaiming forgiveness. He further tells of Jesus's death by crucifixion and then of God raising Jesus from the dead. Peter emphasizes that he was an eyewitness to these events. However, he includes himself among other witnesses when he says, "made him manifest, not to all the people but to us who were chosen by God as witnesses, who ate and drank with him after he rose from the dead" (Acts 10:40–41).

Read that again: "not to all." Reader, you and I are not eyewitnesses, but we proclaim the eyewitness testimony of those who "ate and drank with him after he rose from the dead" (Acts 10:40). For many modern Evangelicals, they long to tell some eyewitness testimony of their experiences, be they about conversion or some charismatic event. However, Peter is clear that the apostles and evangelists are the eyewitnesses, and Christians since have borne their testimony in proclaiming Jesus died, buried, and risen again, according to the Scriptures. *They are eyewitnesses*, and contemporary Christians proclaim what they saw and wrote down for us. Our message is what the apostles and evangelists proclaimed: the forgiveness of sins to all who believe in Jesus Christ the risen One.

The message we are to share is Jesus who died and is risen from the dead. Gregory of Nyssa writes that this is "death's obliteration,"[4] which becomes a "shared benefit and grace"[5] to all who believe. Jesus was not raised by another, like he himself did for Lazarus, but instead, the "only begotten himself raises himself up," proving that our sins are forgiven.

A fascinating part of this sermon is that the apostle Peter offers real, tangible proof of the resurrection when he explains that Jesus ate and drank with them after the resurrection. It is curious that this is added to the recounting of the historic event, because

---

4. Gregory of Nyssa, quoted in Martin and Oden, *Acts*, 135.
5. Gregory of Nyssa, quoted in Martin and Oden, *Acts*, 137.

The One Who Died and Now Lives Gives Life

Jesus, in a glorified body, would no longer need food and drink to live. Severus of Antioch writes,

> After the resurrection he (Jesus) did not need to eat or drink anymore, but only as one believed in by and as one giving evidence to his intimate disciples. Another reason, of which Didymus, Severus, Irenaeus, Chrysostom and Gregory of Nyssa all join together in unity, for this account of Jesus' eating and drinking is that it proved Jesus was not a ghost or spirit.[6]

Rather, it proved Jesus rose again in his physical body, which suffered greatly on the cross and arose "in a divine way." When you are sharing with the unbeliever that Jesus is risen from the dead, it is not as a vision, a ghost or spirit, or some non-corporeal manner, but in his physical body. This is a physical resurrection, not an ethereal one. Jesus conquered death in his physical body, which had suffered and died on the Roman cross of execution. This is the believers' hope, that we too will rise, in these bodies, on that great day when Jesus returns to judge the living and the dead.

This is the message we are to proclaim: Jesus died, was buried, and rose again from the dead on the third day. This is the gospel, which Scripture says is "the power of God unto salvation." Do you long for family, friends, neighbors, co-workers, and others in your social circle to come to Christ and be forgiven, so they too may have eternal life? If you are a Christian, this is your desire. Therefore, even if your own conversion may start the conversation, get off of it as quickly as possible and on to that which saves: the gospel. Prayerfully speak this peace to them, the forgiveness of sins for all who believe in Jesus. Prayerfully look for more opportunities to proclaim and defend the faith, but do so using the pattern set by the apostles and evangelists for *they were eyewitnesses* of these things.

---

6. Severus of Antioch, quoted in Martin and Oden, *Acts*, 137.

10

Not Done in a Corner

Sermon #6 (Part 1): **The Apostle Paul's Proclamation** (Acts 13:16-22)

> So Paul stood up, and motioning with his hand said:
> "Men of Israel and you who fear God, listen. The God of this people Israel chose our fathers and made the people great during their stay in the land of Egypt, and with uplifted arm he led them out of it. And for about forty years he put up with them in the wilderness. And after destroying seven nations in the land of Canaan, he gave them their land as an inheritance. All this took about 450 years. And after that he gave them judges until Samuel the prophet. Then they asked for a king, and God gave them Saul the son of Kish, a man of the tribe of Benjamin, for forty years. And when he had removed him, he raised up David to be their king, of whom he testified and said, 'I have found in David the son of Jesse a man after my heart, who will do all my will.' Of this man's offspring God has brought to Israel a Savior, Jesus, as he promised."

WE NOW MOVE ON to the apostle Paul, who while not an eyewitness of the events at that time, nevertheless saw the risen Jesus Christ on the road to Damascus and then, not taught by man but by revelation by Jesus Christ himself, learned the gospel (Acts 9 and Gal 1:11–12). Paul consistently references the apostles and others' eyewitness testimony throughout his letters, especially 1 Cor 15:3–10. He speaks of Jesus appearing to him, "as to one untimely born." Paul is as much an eyewitness to the risen savior as are Peter, John, James, Mary, and the other five hundred eyewitnesses.

As we look at Paul's sermon, we should ask, "Where does Paul begin?" Paul does not begin his sermon to the Jews gathered in the synagogue in Antioch. Instead, Paul begins with the prophets of old.

> Notice how Paul weaves his discourse from things present and from the prophets . . . the apostles as witnesses of the resurrection, and David bearing witness. For neither do the Old Testament proofs seem so cogent when taken by themselves, or the later testimonies apart from the former. Therefore, it is through both that he makes his discourse trustworthy.[1]

Paul begins with the Old Testament, because it does not make sense unless it is in light of the historical life, death, burial, and resurrection of Jesus. However, he does not begin with the events either, because they must be grounded in the prophetic Scriptures. Using both the Old Testament (prophecies) along with the New Testament (fulfillment of prophecies) may be just where we need to begin as well with the person questioning why we believe. Some have a bit of knowledge about the prophets of old and a little bit about Jesus. Therefore, we should tie these together just as the apostles and evangelists do when the creed which Paul references (see 1 Cor 15) states "according to the Scriptures." The Scriptures Paul references are the Old Testament books of Moses (law) and the prophets, which Jesus said to the men on the road to Emmaus after his resurrection concern him (Luke 24:27).

Today's Christians may find it surprising that Paul utilizes the same pattern for gospel proclamation and the defense of the faith. Why didn't he speak about his road-to-Damascus experience?

---

1. Chrysostom, quoted in Martin and Oden, *Acts*, 163.

Why not tell them of his visions? Simple. Paul understood that the power of God for salvation lies in the gospel, not his experiences. We Christians must remember this fact.

Paul, speaking to Israelites, references the prophets of old and then the gospel accounts of Jesus's life as proof that Jesus is the Savior. Paul, at this point, focuses on the Old Testament prophecies which have been fulfilled in Jesus. Note well that Paul does not recount his experience on the road to Damascus, though he will later. Again, the emphasis is on the gospel message and not even on an apostle's experience. Christians would be well served to remember this pattern and move from their experience to the gospel quickly in their proclamation and defense of the faith. Join with Paul as he emphasizes the prophecies of old coming to fulfillment in Jesus Christ. With the apostle Paul, let us point to Jesus as the Savior which was promised.

Sermon #6 (Part 2): **The Apostle Paul's Proclamation (Acts 13:26–33)**

> "Brothers, sons of the family of Abraham, and those among you who fear God, to us has been sent the message of this salvation. For those who live in Jerusalem and their rulers, because they did not recognize him nor understand the utterances of the prophets, which are read every Sabbath, fulfilled them by condemning him. And though they found in him no guilt worthy of death, they asked Pilate to have him executed. And when they had carried out all that was written of him, they took him down from the tree and laid him in a tomb. But God raised him from the dead, and for many days he appeared to those who had come up with him from Galilee to Jerusalem, who are now his witnesses to the people. And we bring you the good news that what God promised to the fathers, this he has fulfilled to us their children by raising Jesus, as also it is written in the second psalm,
>
> "'You are my Son,
> today I have begotten you.'"

Paul, by appealing to the written Word of God, the promises and prophecies of old, argues for the resurrection of Jesus as an objective truth. He tells them that the rulers didn't recognize Jesus, even though they read the Scriptures each and every Sabbath day. However, just because they missed it doesn't mean it is not true. In fact, Paul defends the faith by going right to the death of Jesus as fulfillment of those very Scriptures. Paul reminds them that Jesus was completely dead and needed burial, so he was laid in a tomb. This is a recounting of what the apostles wrote in the gospel and of what was publically known at the time. "But God raised him from the dead" is the pronouncement of the gospel to the Jews and gentiles in Paul's audience. Jesus's resurrection as fulfillment of the prophecies is also Paul's pattern, just as it is Peter's and must be our own.

In vv. 32–33 we read what the good news is: "what God promised to the fathers, this he has fulfilled to us their children by raising Jesus." Paul does not say the good news is some personal ecstatic experience, tongues, prophecy, dreams, and visions. No. Paul proclaims Jesus's life, death, and resurrection based upon the authoritative written Word of God and the eyewitness account of the apostles themselves as the good news to be proclaimed and defended. That good news is the promises of God fulfilled. Through the use of the Old Testament and the testimony of the eyewitnesses of the fulfillment, namely the apostles' accounts, Paul declares salvation to those to whom he is preaching. Once again, we read the focus is on the objective and verifiable truth of the resurrection and not on Paul's personal testimony.

What was Paul's persuasive argument? Was it that a light brightly shone around him on his way to Damascus? What it that Jesus appeared to him in his resurrection glory? Was it that he was literally blinded and had to be led by the hand to a house until another came to heal him? Was it even that he received healing and his sight back? Not at all. Paul never focuses on his own experiences. Instead, Paul keeps to the actual good news, the gospel account, which tells us that Jesus actually died, was buried, and rose again from the dead, according to the Scriptures. As Paul writes early in his evangelistic and pastoral ministry, his pattern follows that of the other apostles.

We see this pattern clearly when we read what St. Paul writes in 1 Cor 15 as he explains "mere Christianity." Jesus died, according to the Scriptures; Jesus rose again, according to the Scriptures. This is the pattern of New Testament proclamation. Not Paul nor Stephen nor Peter, as shown above, used their personal experiences as proof nor as the message they were to bring to those dying in sin. If the early church used this pattern, how much more should we?

If forgiveness is given because Jesus died for our sins and God raised him from the dead, how much more should we be emphasizing this gospel: Jesus died, was buried, and on the third day rose, according to the Scriptures. What damage do we bring to the proclamation if we base it upon our own subjective experiences rather than the objective truth in the prophets and apostles? We must follow the evangelists and apostles' pattern found in the Scriptures, which shows that we go to the Word of God and proclaim that Jesus died for the forgiveness of all our sins. Always remember that we did not witness these events, but we do have documented testimonials, because *they were eyewitnesses.*

11

To the World

Proclamation to the Gentiles

THUS FAR THE SERMONS of the apostles to Jews and believing gentiles (those who had previously converted to Judaism) has been focused upon. However, what is the pattern when the apostles broaden their proclamation to those of the pagan world: gentiles? Do the apostles follow a pattern as described above, which Peter, Stephen, and Paul used: an objective gospel? Or, does it suddenly change, so that their own personal experiences and subjectivism is the focal point of their sermons, proclamation, and apologetic style?

In Acts 15 we have the issues of how the church is to deal with gentile converts. James, now a believer because of the resurrection of Jesus, references the prophets, who foretold that gentiles too would believe in Jesus. Even within a church issue—whom we accept as believers and what is to be done with gentiles in the church now—James references fulfillment of prophecy.

One of the Scriptures' texts often used for missionary endeavors is Paul's sermon in Acts 17. In my training with Wycliffe Bible Translators, this was the go-to sermon to see how to interact with those who had never before heard the gospel in foreign lands. We were taught to follow Paul's pattern in proclaiming "Jesus saves" to the unconverted. However, recalling that training, we were encouraged to share with others our personal experiences. Sadly, the emphasis remained upon our own salvation testimony and what happened when we believed.

However, Paul does not do that with the Athenians. It is right to say that Paul sticks with the basics and "mere Christianity," for he does not talk to them of visions, dreams, personal prophecies, or the gifts he received, but instead proclaims Christ and him crucified and risen from the dead.

Sermon #7: **The Apostle Paul's Proclamation to Gentiles (Acts 17:22–28)**

> And they took him and brought him to the Areopagus, saying, "May we know what this new teaching is that you are presenting? For you bring some strange things to our ears. We wish to know therefore what these things mean." Now all the Athenians and the foreigners who lived there would spend their time in nothing except telling or hearing something new.
>
> So Paul, standing in the midst of the Areopagus, said: "Men of Athens, I perceive that in every way you are very religious. For as I passed along and observed the objects of your worship, I found also an altar with this inscription: 'To the unknown god.' What therefore you worship as unknown, this I proclaim to you. The God who made the world and everything in it, being Lord of heaven and earth, does not live in temples made by man, nor is he served by human hands, as though he needed anything, since he himself gives to all mankind life and breath and everything. And he made from one man every nation of mankind to live on all the face of the earth, having determined allotted periods and the boundaries of their dwelling place, that they should seek God, and perhaps feel their way toward him and find him. Yet he is actually not far from each one of us, for
>
> > "'In him we live and move and have our being';
> > as even some of your own poets have said,

"'For we are indeed his offspring.'

"Being then God's offspring, we ought not to think that the divine being is like gold or silver or stone, an image formed by the art and imagination of man. The times of ignorance God overlooked, but now he commands all people everywhere to repent, because he has fixed a day on which he will judge the world in righteousness by a man whom he has appointed; and of this he has given assurance to all by raising him from the dead."

Now when they heard of the resurrection of the dead, some mocked. But others said, "We will hear you again about this." So Paul went out from their midst. But some men joined him and believed, among whom also were Dionysius the Areopagite and a woman named Damaris and others with them.

"This I proclaim to you!"

What is the "this" which we are to proclaim? The gospel: Jesus died and rose again for the forgiveness of sins, according to the Scriptures.

While Paul utilizes the writings of their own poets and philosophers, he does not remain there. The apostle Paul, using the religion the people had, false though it was, uses it to turn it "on its head,"[1] as Chrysostom writes. St. Paul utilizes their own understanding that they did not know the true God. Of course, they were just covering their bases, but Paul uses it to springboard into a gospel proclamation. In his doing so, they remain open to listening, and then Paul defeats them by their own false god.

What does this tell us as Christians today? We should be reading the works of others, as Dr. John Warwick Montgomery admonishes every one of his students to be "widely read." Why? If we understand their worldview, we know better its inconsistencies, its falsehoods, and those small bits that retain a "knowledge of God" because God has put "eternity in their hearts" (Eccl. 3:11).

By using what their favorite authors and poets, philosophers and sages, wrote, Paul is reminding them that they are God's offspring. However, though they are God's creation, they do not yet

---

1. Chrysostom, quoted in Martin and Oden, *Acts,* 218.

know God as Father Almighty and therefore themselves as true children of God, and so Paul immediately calls them to repentance through Jesus Christ, because he was the One, the man God appointed, who died and rose again from the dead. This is Paul's message and must be ours. Note well that the apostle did not recount his own personal experiences, his conversion testimony, his healing from blindness after encountering Jesus. Instead, Paul references the resurrection from the dead. His gospel proclamation is that Jesus died and rose again.

Paul does not proclaim an experience of some subjective opinion or feeling. Paul proclaims the one true God and Jesus Christ who is risen from the dead. Paul's style of proclamation is as follows: logical argument, then God and who he really is, and finally repentance and salvation through the death and resurrection of Jesus Christ. "This I proclaim to you!" This we are to proclaim as well. Paul invites them "through the risen Christ, into the abundant mercy of God."[2] He does not call them into some subjective experience but into actual forgiveness of their sins through the actual and verifiable resurrection of Jesus Christ. The resurrection is objectively true and because it is verifiable, through numerous eyewitnesses, they are being offered the forgiveness of their sins.

What is Paul's focus? As he says in his farewell address to the leaders of the churches in Ephesus, it is to testify to the gospel of the grace of God (Acts 20:24). The apostles had no other message than Jesus died, according to the Scriptures, and rose again, according to the Scriptures. They never focused upon their own testimony. In fact, as shown here, if they did refer to their personal experience, it was always in light of their objective testimony of the physical and verifiable resurrection of Jesus Christ after dying and being buried.

> Being then God's offspring, we ought not to think that the divine being is like gold or silver or stone, an image formed by the art and imagination of man. The times of ignorance God overlooked, but now he commands all people everywhere to repent, because he has fixed a day

2. Stromateis, quoted in Martin and Oden, *Acts*, 218.

To the World

on which he will judge the world in righteousness by a man whom he has appointed; and of this he has given assurance to all by raising him from the dead."

Now when they heard of the resurrection of the dead, some mocked. But others said, "We will hear you again about this." So Paul went out from their midst. But some men joined him and believed, among whom also were Dionysius the Areopagite and a woman named Damaris and others with them.

The apostle Paul does a lot of correcting and instructing in this part of his sermon. First, he reminds them that God is not made by human hands, wood, stone, precious metals, but, rather, man is made by the hand of God. Second, Paul teaches them that they are ignorant of the one true God, and now the gracious Lord of all offers to them the forgiveness of sins and calls them to repent of their idolatry. No longer can they claim ignorance, for the message of the resurrection has gone out to the world. Third, Paul exhorts them to receive the gift of forgiveness through Jesus Christ, because he is coming back to judge the living and the dead.

As Chrysostom affirms, "They are being invited, through the risen Christ, into the abundant mercy of God through this change of mind and heart from their previous conceptions of divinity."[3] What a glorious message of forgiveness, new life, and the life everlasting Paul is proclaiming! This is our message as well to those in other religions following false gods, relying upon false hope.

In these passages—and there are many other sermons in Acts that have not been looked at—the pattern is clear: an objective gospel proclamation over and above a subjective presentation. What are we to learn through these passages? It is my hope and prayer that Evangelicals and charismatics will realign their presentation of the gospel with that which is the real gospel: Jesus died and rose again for the forgiveness of sins to all who believe. Again and again it has been shown that Peter, Stephen, James, and Paul all brought in the written Word of God, the prophecies fulfilled, the life and death of Jesus, and his resurrection as witnessed to by their own

---

3. Chrysostom, quoted in Martin and Oden, *Acts,* 221.

eyes and that of several hundred of his disciples. While testimony or miracle may be a starting point it is never *the* point of their message. Always, the proclamation and defense of Christianity, for the apostles and others in the Bible, is the life, death, and resurrection of Jesus. That is where they begin and end. That is where we begin and end:

The gospel is the power of God unto salvation.

12

Recovering the Apostles' Apologetic

Rejecting a Debilitated Gospel and Embracing a Biblical Presentation

IN THIS BOOK, AN attempt has been made to correct an unbalanced situation amongst Evangelicals and charismatics which teaches Christians to emphasize either their own personal testimony or subjective experiences. In restoring an objective guide outside of man himself—the fulfillment of prophecy and the biblical accounts of the eyewitnesses to the physical life, death, and resurrection of Jesus—it is hoped that there will be a restoring equilibrium to religious life. The Bible is the objective guide to proclaiming and defending the faith. Should one resort to one's own personal experiences, it would debilitate the gospel. The gospel is not about you and me, except in the sense that we need it as well. Rather, the gospel is about Jesus and is found most perfectly in the written Word of God. That is where we should start and end any conversation about the forgiveness of sins with those who do not know him. We are to be about proclaiming him and not ourselves, for he is "declared to be the Son of God in power according to the Spirit of holiness by his resurrection from the dead" (Rom 1:4). This is the gospel which is the power of God unto salvation for all who believe (Rom 1:16).

They Were Eyewitnesses

The Bible as the Self-Authenticated Word of God Alone

Having reviewed the religious trends, we see clearly that true religion, which involves man's relation to a Supreme Being, must be guided by this Supreme Being, and this guidance must be tested by some standard outside of man's emotional experience. In other words, if there is a God whom we worship and whom we serve, he must be above and beyond ourselves and prevent each one from thinking his own analytical mind or ecstatic emotion to be supreme.

> Man must be given an objective standard outside of himself by which he may test his subjective spiritual emotions or his philosophies of life and thus protect him from erroneous concepts. If man must be allowed freedom to think, then a God who is supreme and over us and all-wise must have the freedom and authority to give guidance to that thinking in harmony with His superior knowledge. There must be divine inspiration tested by time and experience. Otherwise man would be cast on a sea of despair, and he could only cry out, "Where am I? What is truth?" And only his own echo would answer. If we worship God we must expect this; yea, we must demand this of Him, or man becomes his own god, with himself the supreme being.[1]

The Reformation made an attempt to correct this unbalanced situation by again restoring an objective guide outside of man himself and thus restoring equilibrium to religious life. The Bible became the objective guide, and the subjective spiritual life led people in obedience to its precepts. Saintes has depicted it as follows:

> The spiritual grounds on which the reformers relied to impress on their labors the seal of immortality, and to secure for them the regard even of those who could not agree with them, were their respect for the Scriptures of the Old and New Testaments, which they considered as inspired by the Spirit of God himself.[2]

---

1. Christensen, "Subjective and Objective Religion (Part 1)."
2. Amand Saintes, quoted in Meister, *Building Belief*, 144.

Luther and the Scriptures

> Whoever believes and hold to Christ's Word, heaven stands open to him, hell is shut, the devil is imprisoned, sins are forgiven and he is a child of eternal life. That is what this book teaches you—the Holy Scripture—and no other book on earth.[3]

If Christians are to both proclaim and defend the gospel, it is the Scriptures we must use. If we are to proclaim the whole counsel of God, then it is the content of that gospel (Jesus died, was buried, and rose again) that we must consistently use. As Martin Luther states clearly, this book teaches you, and then God uses you to teach the unbeliever and skeptic what the good news truly is. This echoes the apostle Paul when he writes that faith comes through hearing, and hearing through the Word of God (Rom 10), and that you are needed to speak this truth to those who do not know Christ as Lord and Savior. Nowhere does God tell us to tell our personal testimony. Instead, God says the gospel is the power unto salvation (Rom 1:16–17).

The following sample quotations from Luther could be duplicated from the other Reformers: "Scripture alone is the true lord and master of all writings and doctrine on earth."[4] "God's will is completely contained therein, so that we must constantly go back to them. Nothing should be presented which is not confirmed by the authority of both Testaments and agrees with them."[5] "Know, then, that the Old Testament is a book of laws, which teaches what men are to do and not to do . . . just as the New Testament is a gospel or book of grace, and teaches where one is to get the power to fulfill the law."[6] Each quote here speaks of how God uses the Scriptures, not your personal testimony, to bring faith to

---

3. Luther, WA 48:155, quoted in Van Nest, "Luther on the Value."

4. Luther, quoted in Silverdale Lutheran Church, "Luther or Lutheran Quotes."

5. Luther, quoted in North American Lutheran Church, "Weekly Commentary."

6. Luther, quoted in Yale Bible Study, "Reformation History."

individuals. God chose to use the means of grace to dispense salvation, and we have no right to try any other method, no matter how enticing it might be. God's evangelists and apostles were the eyewitnesses, and we bring their testimony to bear as we proclaim and defend the faith.

The Reformation was a restoration of faith based on something outside of people (means of grace/sacraments), and yet the Reformers were strongly moved from within. They went back to the foundation of the early church. But this did not continue long. The spiritual force was soon lost, the objective guide was dimmed, and many controversies arose. It seems to be the pitfall of every generation to rely upon their own personal experience, subjectivism, and testimonies to proclaim the gospel, instead of using the pattern set forth in the Scriptures. To quote Saintes:

> Luther and Melancthon were hardly in their graves before the theologians of their school set to work, though indirectly, to destroy the fruits of their masters' labours. New hair-splitting controversies arose too numerous to mention. They had lost their inner spiritual experience and with it their objective standard. They had lost their subjective-objective balance. Hurst says, "There could be but one moral result to the prolonged strife—a great, spiritual decline."[7]

The pattern for proclaiming and defending the gospel has been clearly shown by the apostles. First, they appeal to Scripture and the fulfillment of hundreds of prophecies in the Old Testament. Second, they talk about what they eyewitnessed personally, it having occurred "within their own personal knowledge."[8] Third, they speak of Jesus as being a real man who lived, died, was buried, and rose again from the dead, according to the Scriptures. These men, the apostles upon whom the pillars of the church, along with the prophets, are founded, with Christ as chief cornerstone, focus their message upon these things every time we look at their sermons. Before religious leaders, prison guards, gentile converts to

---

7. Christensen, "Subjective and Objective Religion."
8. Greenleaf, "Testimony of the Evangelists."

Judaism, followers of other religions and rulers, the apostles proclaim Christ crucified and risen from the dead. This is the gospel message: the forgiveness of sins through Jesus Christ.

As Christians some two thousand years later, we have no new message, no new light to bring. The apostles' message that Jesus died, was buried, and rose again, is our message. We have their testimony to the truths of what actually and historically took place. We have their word in the Word of God, and that is what we are to proclaim. We should not look for new presentations when the one in Scripture is itself the power of God unto salvation. Friend, do you desire that sinners come to Christ and receive the forgiveness of sins and eternal life? Then move away from your own experiences and testimony and back to the testimony of the apostles. You are not an eyewitness to the life, death, burial, and resurrection of Jesus, though certainly that truth has brought you to true faith. Instead, we are to carry the message that they proclaimed because . . .

They were eyewitnesses.

Epilogue

"The Harvest Is Great but the Laborers Are Few"

SINCE MY CONVERSION TO Christianity I have longed for unbelievers and skeptics alike to come to true faith and have their sins forgiven as well. This is my passion, as well as to pass this desire along to other Christians, so they too can proclaim and defend the faith. Calvinistic doctrine, with its emphasis on God choosing some to salvation and sending others directly to hell with no possibility of coming to faith, in its practice nearly snuffed this desire out completely. My old Pentecostalism and charismatic life, well, it was all about telling my personal experiences and getting the person to make a decision or pray the sinner's prayer. However, now with understanding the plain reading of Scripture, this desire to proclaim and defend the Christian faith has once again burst into a roaring fire.

Augustine says, "Zeal without knowledge is a dangerous thing."[1] That still holds true, even as a Lutheran. This is true for all Christians. Therefore, if we can look into the Scripture passages, reading and studying those sermons given by the apostles, we will learn better how to defend the faith. Then perhaps that will fan the flames to proclaim and defend the faith around you.

As Scripture teaches, the harvest is great but the laborers are few (Luke 10:2). Christians are to labor in the vocations to which

---

1 Augustine, quoted in Coakley and Sterk, *Earliest Christianity to 1453*, 199.

God has called them. As we serve and love God by serving and loving our neighbors, each of us comes into contact with unbelievers and skeptics regularly. It is my hope that by having read and gone through this book and the sermons from the evangelists and apostles contained in it, you will have been encouraged to step away from your old way of sharing the gospel via personal testimony and instead use the pattern God has given us. If just one person reading this book makes that change, then I will have been successful in my endeavor. May God grant us grace and mercy.

It is my heart's desire that Christians everywhere are ready and prepared to answer for their faith, using the testimony of the apostles and evangelists in the Gospels and book of Acts. If you want to learn more about apologetics and become better equipped to respond to their questions about the Christian faith, I invite you to join me and a wonderful group of Christians every Monday at 2 p.m. (Mountain Time) online for #ApologeticsTogether. Please contact me either on the contact form at my website (www.lutherangirl.org) or via email at drnancyalmodovar@gmail.com.

> In your hearts honor Christ the Lord as holy, always being prepared to make a defense to anyone who asks you for a reason for the hope that is in you; yet do it with gentleness and respect. (1 Pet 3:15)

Resources

Ackley, A. H. "I Serve a Risen Savior." https://hymnary.org/text/i_serve_a_risen_savior.
Almodovar, Nancy A. *A Modern Ninety-Five: Questions Today's Evangelicals Need to Answer.* Eugene, OR: Resource, 2008.
Bente, Gerhard Friedrich. *Historical Introductions to the Lutheran Confessions.* 2nd ed. St. Louis: Concordia, 2005.
Bergendoff, Conrad John Immanuel. *The Church of the Lutheran Reformation: A Historical Survey of Lutheranism.* Saint Louis: Concordia, 1967.
Blumhofer, Edith L. *Aimee Semple McPherson: Everybody's Sister.* Library of Religious Biography. Grand Rapids: Eerdmans, 1993.
———. *The Assemblies of God: A Chapter in the Story of American Pentecostalism.* 2 vols. Springfield, MO: Gospel, 1989.
———. *The Assemblies of God: A Popular History.* Springfield, MO: Radiant, 1985.
———. *"Pentecost in My Soul": Explorations in the Meaning of Pentecostal Experience in the Assemblies of God.* Springfield, MO: Gospel, 1989.
———. *Restoring the Faith: The Assemblies of God, Pentecostalism, and American Culture.* Urbana, IL: University of Illinois Press, 1993.
Blumhofer, Edith L., and Randall Balmer, eds. *Modern Christian Revivals.* Urbana, IL: University of Illinois Press, 1993.
Blumhofer, Edith L., Russell P. Spittler, and Grant A. Wacker, eds. *Pentecostal Currents in American Protestantism.* Urbana, IL: University of Illinois Press, 1999.
Brown, Harold O. J. *Heresies: Heresy and Orthodoxy in the History of the Church.* Peabody, MA: Hendrickson, 1998.
Bruner, Frederick Dale. *A Theology of the Holy Spirit: The Pentecostal Experience and the New Testament Witness.* Grand Rapids: Eerdmans, 1970.
Burfeind, Peter M. *Gnostic America: A Reading of Contemporary American Culture and Religion According to Christianity's Oldest Heresy.* Toledo: Pax Domini, 2014.
Chantry, Walter J. *Signs of the Apostles: Observations on Pentecostalism Old and New.* Carlisle, PA: Banner of Truth, 1976.

Resources

Chemnitz, Martin. *The Two Natures of Christ*. Translated by J. A. O. Preus. Vol. 6 of *Chemnitz's Works*. St. Louis: Concordia, 2007.

Christian Truths Summarized: The Creeds and Reformed Confessions. n.p.: United Reformed Church, 2011.

Christensen, Otto H. "Subjective and Objective Religion (Concluded)." *Ministry International Journal for Pastors* (Dec. 1965). https://www.ministrymagazine.org/archive/1965/12/subjective-and-objective-religion.

———. "Subjective and Objective Religion (Part 1)." *Ministry International Journal for Pastors* (Nov. 1965). https://www.ministrymagazine.org/archive/1965/11/subjective-and-objective-religion.

Clement, Arthur J. *The Evangelicals and Charismatics: A Confessional Lutheran Evaluation*. Impact. Milwaukee: Northwestern, 2000.

———. *Pentecost or Pretense?: An Examination of the Pentecostal and Charismatic Movements*. Milwaukee: Northwestern, 1981.

Coakley, John W. and Andrea Sterk. *Earliest Christianity to 1453*. Vol. 1 of *Readings in World Christian History*. Maryknoll, NY: Orbis, 2004.

Collver, Albert. "Luther's Invocavit Sermons." *Twelfth International Congress for Luther Research* (Aug. 2012) 57–67.

Commission on Worship of the Lutheran Church—Missouri Synod. *Lutheran Service Book*. St. Louis: Concordia, 2006.

Copan, Paul. *How Do You Know You're Not Wrong?: Responding to Objections That Leave Christians Speechless*. Grand Rapids: Baker Books, 2005.

Cox, Harvey. *Fire from Heaven: The Rise of Pentecostal Spirituality and the Reshaping of Religion in the Twenty-First Century*. Reading, MA: Addison-Wesley, 1995.

Dallimore, Arnold A. *Forerunner of the Charismatic Movement: The Life of Edward Irving*. Carlisle, PA: Banner of Truth, 1983.

Davies, Paul Ewing. "An Examination of the Views of Edward Irving Concerning the Person and Work of Jesus Christ." PhD diss., New College, 1928.

Davis, William. "Why I Am No Longer a Pentecostal." June–July–Aug. 2013. http://www.oldpaths.com/Archive/Davis/William/Charles/Jr/1952/Pentecostalism.html.

Dorries, David W. *Edward Irving's Incarnational Christology*. N.p.: Xulon, 2002.

Douthat, Ross. *Bad Religion: How We Became a Nation of Heretics*. New York: Free, 2012.

Eckhardt, John. *Moving in the Apostolic: God's Plan to Lead His Church to the Final Victory*. Ventura, CA: Renew, 1999.

Edgar, William, and K. Scott Oliphint, eds. "Tertullian (ca. 160–225)." In *Christian Apologetics Past and Present: A Primary Source Reader*, 1:117. Wheaton, IL: Crossway 2009.

Engelbrecht, Edward A., et al., eds. *Church History: The Basics*. Abridged ed. of *The Church from Age to Age*. St. Louis: Concordia, 2016.

"Epistle for the Day: 1 Corinthians 1:1–9." Bulletin insert for *Lesson 12: Second Sunday after Epiphany*. St. Louis: Concordia Publishing House, 2009.

Resources

Eusebius. *The History of the Church: From Christ to Constantine*. Translated by G. A. Williamson. Baltimore: Penguin, 1965.

Fisk, Jonathan. *Broken: Seven "Christian" Rules That Every Christian Ought to Break as Often as Possible*. St. Louis: Concordia, 2012.

Gardiner, Gordon P. *Out of Zion into All the World*. Ridgewood, NY: Destiny Image, 1990.

Gill, Kenneth. "Dividing over Oneness." https://www.christianitytoday.com/history/issues/issue-58/dividing-over-oneness.html.

Greenleaf, Simon. "Testimony of the Evangelists." https://www.famous-trials.com/jesustrial/1051-evangeliststestimony.

Halverson, Marvin, and Arthur A. Cohen, eds. *A Handbook of Christian Theology: Definition Essays on Concepts and Movements of Thought in Contemporary Protestantism*. Cleveland: World, 1958.

Halvorson, T R. *Catechetical Evangelism in the Newspaper*. N.p., 2017.

Harrup, Scott. "A Pentecostal Look at Christmas." *Pentecostal Evangel*, Dec. 25, 2011. https://news.ag.org/en/News/A-Pentecostal-Look-at-Christmas?fbclid=IwAR0hvgY5y-hi_EGSlVusUzt5c1ssM_xli11R7g3a5KYcZKO8JKqQcQVEcV0.

Masius, Hector Gottfried. *A Defense of the Lutheran Faith on the Eve of Modern Times*. Edited and translated by John Warwick Montgomery. Milwaukee: Northwestern, 2016.

Hoover, Arlie J. *Don't You Believe It!* Chicago: Moody, 1982.

Jacobsen, Douglas. *Thinking in the Spirit: Theologies of the Early Pentecostal Movement*. Bloomington, IN: Indiana University Press, 2003.

Judisch, Douglas. *An Evaluation of Claims to the Charismatic Gifts*. Grand Rapids: Baker, 1978.

Koehler, Edward W. A. *A Summary of Christian Doctrine: A Popular Presentation of the Teachings of the Bible*. 3rd ed. St. Louis: Concordia, 2006.

Kolb, Robert. *The Christian Faith: A Lutheran Exposition*. St. Louis: Concordia, 1993.

Koukl, Gregory. *Tactics: A Game Plan for Discussing Your Christian Convictions*. Grand Rapids: Zondervan, 2009.

Lecky, William Edward Hartpole. *History of the Rise and Influence of the Spirit of Rationalism in Europe*. 2 vols. New York: Appleton, 1925.

Lehman, Roger. "Come Unto Jesus." Three-part sermon given at Evangel Church, Long Island City, NY, Feb., 2011.

Lindberg, Carter. *Third Reformation: Charismatic Movements and the Lutheran Tradition*. Macon, GA: Mercer University Press, 1983.

Lueker, Erwin L., ed. *Lutheran Cyclopedia*. Saint Louis: Concordia, 1954.

Luther, Martin. "Against the Heavenly Prophets." In *Luther's Works*, edited by Jaroslav Pelikan and Helmut T. Lehmann, 40:213–15. Saint Louis: Concordia Pub. House, 1955.

———. "Church and Ministry." In *Luther's Works*, edited by Jaroslav Pelikan and Helmut T. Lehmann, 40:40–41. Saint Louis: Concordia Pub. House, 1955.

Resources

———. "Lord, Keep Us Steadfast in Your Word." Edited by the Commission on Worship of the Lutheran Church—Missouri Synod. Translated by Catherine Winkworth. #655 in *Lutheran Service Book*. St. Louis: Concordia, 2006.

———. *Selected Writings of Martin Luther*. Edited by Theodore G. Tappert. Philadelphia: Fortress, 1967.

———. *What Luther Says: An Anthology*. Edited by Ewald M. Plass. St. Louis: Concordia, 1959.

MacLeod, Donald. "The Doctrine of the Incarnation in Scottish Theology: Edward Irving." *Scottish Bulletin of Evangelical Theology* (Spring 1991). https://www.biblicalstudies.org.uk/pdf/sbet/09-1_040.pdf.

Martin, Francis and Thomas C. Oden, eds. *Acts*. Ancient Christian Commentary on Scripture (New Testament) 5. Downers Grove, IL: InterVarsity, 2006.

Martin, Sean. *The Cathars: The Most Successful Heresy of the Middle Ages*. N.p.: Chartwell, 2006.

Mayer, Frederick Emanuel. *The Religious Bodies of America*. 4th ed. Saint Louis: Concordia, 1961.

McCain, Paul Timothy, ed. *Concordia: The Lutheran Confessions; A Reader's Edition of the Book of Concord*. Translated by William Hermann Theodore Dau. St. Louis: Concordia, 2005.

McGrath, Alister. *Heresy: A History of Defending the Truth*. New York: HarperOne, 2009.

Meister, Chad V. *Building Belief: Constructing Faith from the Ground Up*. Grand Rapids: Baker, 2006.

Menzies, William W. *Anointed to Serve: The Story of the Assemblies of God*. Springfield, MO: Gospel, 1971.

Montgomery, John Warwick. "Christianity in a Corner." N.p.: 1517 The Legacy Project, 2016. Audio lecture.

———. *Defending the Gospel in Legal Style: Essays on Legal Apologetics and the Justification of Classical Christian Faith*. Christian Philosophy Today. Eugene, OR: Wipf and Stock, 2017.

———. *Defending the Gospel through the Centuries: A History of Christian Apologetics*. Calgary, Can.: Canadian Institute for Law, Theology and Public Policy, 1997.

Montgomery, John Warwick, and Gene Edward Veith, eds. *Where Christ Is Present: A Theology for All Seasons on the Five Hundredth Anniversary of the Reformation*. Irving, CA: NRP, 2015.

Moreland, J. P. *Kingdom Triangle: Recover the Christian Mind, Renovate the Soul, Restore the Spirit's Power*. Grand Rapids: Zondervan, 2007.

———. *Scaling the Secular City: A Defense of Christianity*. Grand Rapids: Baker, 1987.

Neve, J. L. *A History of Christian Thought*. 2 vols. Philadelphia: United Lutheran, 1943–46.

Noll, Mark A., and Edith L. Blumhofer, eds. *Sing Them Over Again to Me: Hymns and Hymnbooks in America*. Religion and American Culture. Tuscaloosa, AL: University of Alabama Press, 2006.

Resources

Noll, Mark A., and David F. Wells, eds. *Christian Faith and Practice in the Modern World: Theology from an Evangelical Point of View*. Grand Rapids: Eerdmans, 1988.

North American Lutheran Church. "Weekly Commentary." https://thenalc.org/reading/daily-reading-january-25-2020/.

Parton, Craig A. *The Defense Never Rests: A Lawyer Among the Theologians*. 2nd ed. St. Louis: Concordia, 2015.

———. *Religion on Trial*. St. Louis: Concordia, 2018.

Pieper, Franz. *Christian Dogmatics*. 4 vols. St. Louis: Concordia, 1950–57.

Pless, John T. *Praying Luther's Small Catechism: The Pattern of Sound Words*. St. Louis: Concordia, 2016.

Richard, Matthew. *Will the Real Jesus Please Stand Up?: Twelve False Christs*. St. Louis: Concordia, 2017.

Robertson, O. Palmer. *Final Word*. Carlisle, PA: Banner of Truth, 1993.

Sasse, Hermann. *We Confess Anthology*. Translated by Norman Nagel. St. Louis: Concordia, 2003.

Sayers, Dorothy L. *Creed or Chaos*. Manchester, NH: Sophia Institute, 1995.

Schaff, Philip. *Creeds of Christendom*. 3 vols. Grand Rapids: Baker, 1996.

———, ed. *A Select Library of the Nicene and Post-Nicene Fathers of the Christian Church*. 2nd ser. Grand Rapids: Eerdmans, 1989–94.

Schiller, Friedrich. *Schiller's Philosophical Letters*. N.p.: Theophania, 2012.

Schmidt, Alvin J. *Hallmarks of Lutheran Identity*. St. Louis: Concordia, 2017.

Shedd, William G. T. *Dogmatic Theology*. 3 vols. Nashville: Thomas Nelson, 1980.

Sherrill, John L. *They Speak with Other Tongues*. Grand Rapids: Chosen, 1985.

Silverdale Lutheran Church. "Luther or Lutheran Quotes on Scripture Alone or Word Alone." https://silverdalelutheran.org/wp-content/uploads/2013/10/Luther-Quotes-on-Scripture-Alone.pdf.

Sire, James W. *Scripture Twisting: Twenty Ways the Cults Misread the Bible*. Downers Grove, IL: InterVarsity, 1980.

Smeaton, George. *The Doctrine of the Holy Spirit*. London: Banner of Truth, 1958.

Strachan, C. Gordon. *The Pentecostal Theology of Edward Irving*. London: Darton, Longman and Todd, 1973.

Sutton, A Trevor. *Clearly Christian: Following Jesus in This Age of Confusion*. St. Louis: Concordia, 2018.

Van Nest, Ray. "Luther on the Value of the Bible." http://rayvanneste.com/?p=542.

Walther, C. F. W. *Law and Gospel: How to Read and Apply the Bible*. St. Louis: Concordia, 2010.

Ward, Rowland S. *Spiritual Gifts in the Apostolic Church: Their Nature, Function and Cessation in the Light of the New Testament Evidence*. Golden Beach, Aus.: Ward, 1972.

Warfield, Benjamin Breckinridge. *Counterfeit Miracles*. London: Banner of Truth, 1995.

Resources

———. *The Inspiration and Authority of the Bible*. Oxford: Benediction Classics, 2017.
Wells, David F., and John D. Woodbridge, eds. *The Evangelicals: What They Believe, Who They Are, Where They Are Changing*. Grand Rapids: Baker Book House, 1977.
Wimber, John. "Spiritual Phenomena: Slain in the Spirit." In *Spiritual Phenomena: Slain in the Spirit*. Ann Arbor, Mich: Vine Books, 1981.
Wolff, Richard. "Against the Heavenly Televangelists: A Lutheran Critique of the Televised Preaching of Joel Osteen and John Hagee." *LOGIA* (October 2015).
Wolfmueller, Bryan. *Has American Christianity Failed*. St. Louis: Concordia Publishing House, 2016.
Yale Bible Study. "Reformation History." https://3lvynv3mei4c241zmx1uzxfd-wpengine.netdna-ssl.com/wp-content/uploads/2019/10/Reformation-History-Genesis-Study-Guide.pdf.

www.ingramcontent.com/pod-product-compliance
Lightning Source LLC
Chambersburg PA
CBHW071159090426
42736CB00012B/2389